PAPER FLOWERS

KIAS EMMANUEL CREECH

LeapWrite Literary
137 Forest Park Lane
NC 27360 USA

Copyright © 2024 by Kias Emmanuel Creech.

ISBN 979-8-89376-137-5 (softcover)
ISBN 979-8-89376-138-2 (ebook)

All rights reserved. No part of this book may be reproduced or transmitted in any form or by any means, electronic or mechanical, including photocopying, recording, or by any information storage and retrieval system without express written permission from the author, except in the case of brief quotations embodied in critical reviews and certain other noncommercial uses permitted by copyright law.

Printed in the United States of America.

Patricia and Kias

An enormous Thank You to my best friend since 1995, my sister, twin of my soul, my inspiration and so much more. You have been so much to me, including a source of hope along life's journey, and I am eternally grateful for you. Each and every one of these Paper Flowers I have picked especially for you to show my gratitude and honor of our friendship through the years and I hope you cherish them all as much as I cherish you. Thank you

TABLE OF CONTENTS

Absent Star 1
Aeron 3
Etain (The Shining One) 5
Golden Leaf 8
In My Heart 9
Ink On A Page 11
"My Prayer" 13
Pictavian Shadows 17
Without Me 19
Just Across The River 20
Condition Of The Heart 22
I Think She's Really An Angel 23
"Window Of My Soul" 25
The Light 26
Transformation 27
Far Behind 28
Hold On 30
Questions 32
Out of Reach 34
White tower 36
9/11 38
Arrow's On Fire 40
Awaiting 41
Book Of Shadows Prayer 42
Broken 43
Cry, wolf 45
Dying Rose 47
Free 49
Hallucinations 50

Hold The Line	51
Inside Your Heart	52
My Search	53
Racing Thought	55
Slipping	56
Somewhere To Run	57
Soon	59
Still	60
Stuart	62
Tears In Heaven	63
Thankful	64
Twin Of My Soul	67
What Wasn't Said	69
Earth Angels	71
Ellarae	72
For You	73
"God's Angel"	75
In The Shadow Of The King	77
Doors	78
Piece Of Heaven	80
Savior	81
The Holly & The Envy	83
Venuka	84
What I Mean	85
Alpine Crystals	87
All I've Ever Known Was You	89
Always (2015)	91
Ann	93
Beautiful You	94
Cone Of Power	96
Cycle	97
Do Not Bend	99
Dream	100

Eclipse	101
Elsa	103
Empty Season	104
Endurance	106
Eternity	107
Everything's Alright	109
Fill	111
Golden Tears	113
"Goodbye"	114
Helen (2015)	116
Higher Love	121
How I Feel	122
I Love You More (2015)	123
I've Got To Feel It	124
If You Must Go	127
Illusion	128
Island	130
Karpathia	132
Karpathia II	135
Like Trees Falling	137
Looking For Something	138
My Love (2015)	139
My Precious Gift	140
My Treasure	141
Never Love One Like You	143
Never Love One Like You II	144
Night Of The Tear	145
None So Blind	147
Outside The Lines	149
Sisters	151
Sleeping	152
Sounds Like The Rain	153
Still Falling	154

Storm Passing 155
Strong Enough 157
Tears 160
The Fall 162
There Is No Distance 164
Think Of You 165
This Love I Have For You.. 167
To Be Near You 168
Vision Of Love 169
Wheel Turning 170
You Are My Love 171
You Only Have To Say You Love Me 172
2 Candles 174
Amayas.. 177
Angel In The Snow 179
Asagalen 181
Ash... 183
Believe In Love 185
Blood On The Moon 187
Breaking 188
Burning Well 190
Casting Stones.. 191
Chains.. 192
Circle And A Chain 194
Colorblind 196
Every Shade Of Blue 198
Face The Rain 200
Free (2016).. 202
Fulfilling Your Wish... 203
Ginny.. 205
Glancing Through Clouds.. 207
Goodbye (2016).. 208
Hearts Across The Ocean 209

Hearts Prayer	210
Hidden	211
Hold On	213
Holding To My Memories	215
How It Feels	216
In Everything, Your Heart	218
Inside Your Eyes	220
Island In The Sky	222
Light In Dark Places	224
Love That Smile	226
Loving You	228
Missing You	230
My Eagle	231
My Sweet Rose	233
On Our Way	234
One Soul	236
One Star	237
Only For You	239
Over The Wall	241
Patricia (2016)	243
Petals On The Ground	245
Picture Of You	247
Red, Red Roses	250
Roses In The Rain	252
Runaway Heart	254
Schizoaffective	256
Search For Light	258
Sometimes It's Just Your Voice	260
Storm	261
Strings	262
Tear Tracks	264
That Night	266
The Beautiful One	268

The Next Big Thing	270
The Rain	272
The Stone	274
Void	276
When Loneliness Dies	277
Where Flowers Don't Die	279
Writer	280
Yellow Light	282
You'll Never Know	284
7 New Worlds	285
At All	287
Because Of You	288
Bleeding Pen (FV)	289
Bleeding Pen (The Rhythm)	290
Companion	292
Complete	293
Dancing Angels	294
Decision	297
Drifting	299
Enter Jakob	300
Final Stage of Love	302
Forever	303
Gift	304
Gratitude	305
Hearts Chain	306
Heaven On Earth	307
I Found You	309
Island Sweets	310
Just So You Know	313
Lights Go Out	314
Lisa	315
More Than You'll Ever Know	316
Mr. Indigo	318

My Rose..321
Prayer For You 323
Scar Upon My Heart 324
Sounds 326
Story..327
Thank you, Lord..331
The Call...332
The Wall..333
To Love You..335
Today...336
Use Me 337
Water...338
What I Feel..341
You 343
Cats In Trees...345
Chasing Shadows 347
Chosen One 349
Desire Of My Heart...350
Emily's Field 352
Final Chapter..354
I'm Loving You..356
If Love Was Just A Color..357
Keep Me Away..359
Our Destiny 360
Out Of My Hands..362
Roses In Chains..363
Sea Of Tears 364
Someone 365
Someone Like You 366
The Journey Home...367
Paper Flowers...369

March 13, 2013

ABSENT STAR

What will I tell my heart
When it asks me where you are
What will I tell its fondest dream
When there's a wish but there's no star

What will I tell its temperament
When it feels at such a loss
What will it do when it comes to the river
But has no bridge to cross

What will I tell the wind
That it used to sail upon
What will I tell its nighttime sky
When there is no coming dawn

What will I tell its storm clouds
When its core is parched for rain
What will I tell the majestic sun
When it cannot pierce through pain

When it looks in to the heavens
To see endless constellations
But only sees a blackened sky
And lonesome confirmations

Or across the endless ocean
At rest or highest tide
And cannot find the place
Where you are on the other side

What will I tell the mountains
With their peaks I cannot see
Why must I have to tell my heart
That without you, there's no me

How will I tell the snow clouds
Too cold to produce a flake
That my heart is their reflection
And it's about to break

There will never be another
To hold the place where you are
My dream, my peace, my nighttime sky
My spirits absent star

2013

AERON
(Arrows on fire - alternate version)

Arrows on fire
Straight from Aeron's bow
Anxiously seeking
The heart of her foe

Waiting to pierce
Drive through & depart
Mortally wounding
Their evil heart

Stripping the spirit
Apart from the bone
Until from deception
Their heart stands alone

No more can they taunt
Nor run from the truth
As its an eye for an eye
And a tooth for a tooth

Defending righteousness
And the fortress of God
Where their unfortunate souls
And feet cannot trod

Nailing black wings
To the solid earth
To make way for bliss
And to peace give birth

Do not be guilty
Of walking the wire
Truth comes to you
And her arrow's on fire

May 9, 2013

ETAIN (THE SHINING ONE)

Her horse was white like a Highlands snow
As she tracked her prey, her eternal foe

With eyes as dark as the coming night
And her black hair streaked with bands of white

A sharpened spear in her strong, right hand
In defense of her people & too, their land

Their home, their solace that for years they'd known
That with working hands, their love they'd shown

Sown like seeds within the earth
Their love of home was given birth

For their children that would someday see
Their home, God made for them to be

At war with people that were "civilized"
Yet only greed shown from their eyes

More power, more fame for generations to acknowledge
With a thirst for blood that could not be abolished

Onward they pressed till soon they invaded
A paradise that would never be jaded

Then onward still this white horse came
To avenge a warrior with unspoken name

That rode upon her mare with pride
As with so called "savages" her heart did bide

Her kings son had been put to death
With his innocence still on his breath

His body discovered & with no words spoken
An ancestral link in the chain was broken

A father had been left to grieve
A king of many who fully believed

That the goddess Etain would ride through the air
With a vengeance she would not need swear

On a foggy mist which she would ride
In honor of the prince who had died

Seeking out all enemies
Casting light on their amenities

With a sword of flames she'd burn them out
Till not one was standing, there was no doubt

When the fight was over & the war was through
Her majesty stayed shining through

When all of enemy blood was shed
And opposition was counted dead

On a Snow White horse in celestial flight
The goddess Etain went home by night

In admiration & heartfelt praise
Toward the skies their eyes were raised

In purity, without one stain
A promise from the Great Etain

"If you ever need me, in your heart I'll be
Even though your eyes may never see

In loyalty & no remorse
I'll ride upon my great white horse

With sword in hand, and shield & spear
Take comfort, I am always near

Not one of your enemies shall remain
For I am your wrath, I am Etain!"

June 30, 2013

GOLDEN LEAF

I bought a brand new blank book
Each page in golden leaf
Each 1 waiting for my thoughts
Emotions & beliefs

Each 1 intimidating
For to me they must be filled
Be it pain or pleasure
Something waits to be revealed

A work as yet unwritten
A feeling yet to shine
Perhaps an invitation
To come drink, be well & dine

A thought that can't be wasted
Or a dream since thrown away
If just simply an "I love you"
There's a message to convey

Or that which has laid in secret
A wish, dream or desire
Maybe that which has yet to be
Like a spark that becomes a fire

So as each page that I'm filling
And with each a sweet relief
I must never waste a letter
In my book with golden leaf

April 24, 2013

IN MY HEART

In my heart, there is a longing
That my mind cannot deny,
A weighted, homesick feeling
And a dream I can't let die!

A promise yet unbroken,
A sign as yet unseen
Is waiting in the distance
To become my fondest dream

To become a wish unspoken
To arise from dark & gloom
And open in great splendor
As a flower in full bloom

A candle in the darkness,
A note as yet unplayed,
A song waiting to be sung
An ancient veil not frayed

Untouched by time & trouble
Seen only by the Light
Waiting to surrender
Like the moon in darkest night

Some day it'll be discovered
Generations soon will see
That which I wanted most in life
Was just your love for me

Your love to me unspoken
As years I've waited still
Hoping that its NOT a dream
And that it's, indeed, real

My hope in that beginning
My faith in that new start
My hunt that's never ending
For your love inside my heart

4-21-2013

INK ON A PAGE

Your birthday is coming, a day I hold dear
It's a day that I wished for when God brought you here.

He placed you in paradise, of this I've no doubt
For from this land, an angel came out

This angel was you & could be no other
Wrapped in divinity, you came as my brother

I didn't know this at first, it took me a while
The fact of Gods majesty, made true by your smile

Made real by your presence, before my eyes
He always presents such a sweet surprise

Out of a battlefield, at the sidelines of peace
Where there's serenity & war cries must cease

Weapons set down as eyes sparkled bright
A family reunion took place that night

I remember it well, July 19
Not a hope, not a wish, but a heartfelt dream

I'm eternally grateful & forever shall be
Celebrating the gift God gave to me

When I stand on the beach & look out 'cross the ocean
I will see an eternal loyalty & devotion

In words I shall write, think, dream or utter
I will always speak highly of you, my brother

Long after everyone's forgotten your age
You will always be more to me than ink on a page!

June 5, 2013 @ 8:21pm

"MY PRAYER"

When I visit you
I feel at peace
All my anxieties
Begin to cease

My soul returns
To times before
My heart walks through
Your open door

A feeling deep
Inside my heart
Comes forth til all else
Must depart

I feel your breath
Each time I pray
Behind me yet
You light my way

The dark, like fog
Begins to fade
In to a place
I cannot evade

A place of peace
And familiarity
A place I know
I need to be

A sacred rite
Each time I come
A blessing that
Cannot be undone

A call that never
Will be quiet
Try as some may
They can't defy it

Some insist
They do not believe
But within me, You
I fully receive

No disbelief
Can be found here
No doubt convinces me
You are not near

No way my voice
Cannot contain
The praises of
Your Holy Name

They ask how I know
As my soul imparts
You live within
My joyous heart

Joyous with a fire
That eternally burns
With a longing for
When you return

To take us children
Beneath your wings
Yet my soul does not
Need such to sing

As it utters words
Of heartfelt praise
And weary arms
Find strength to raise

For I know you live
Every moment I see
Undying love
You have for me

I am not forced
I freely give
With the love I have
And the life I live

For nothing else
Could ever be
The Savior
You have been to me

With all my love
With all my might
With these words
You've let me write

I vow, I promise
Until the end
Your majesty
I shall defend

For all my life
With all my love
I send this promise
Up above

That not of me
But all to you
In all that I say
And all that I do

All adoration
And every thing
I credit to you
My eternal King

June 23, 2013 @ 6:23pm

PICTAVIAN SHADOWS

I visit you often
In my heart & my mind
Still somehow I feel
That I've been left behind

Your legacy lives
And flows through my veins
But there's no sound more lonesome
Than when I speak your name

Time separates us
Though we're brought together
In my heart & my mind
You are with me forever

I visit you often
In thought & in dreams
I'm drawn closer that way
Or at least it seems

I wear your symbols
I fight for your cause
Without hesitation
Regret or pause

Waiting on my investments
That my desire comes true
The long, awaited answer
That I'm 1 with you

No room for doubt
I must look ahead
This passion I breathe
Will never dread...

My confirmation
In the message you've sent
That I am, in fact
Of Pictish descent

My heart then shall soar
High above ground
Where Pictavian shadows
Are abundantly found!

July 9, 2013

WITHOUT ME

When you find yourself & come running back
I'll be as the prey just harder to track

I'll be the leaf upon the wind
I'll be the tree that will not bend

I'll walk through snow, rain or even fire
I'll go to the place of my hearts desire

To every corner of the earth
And to every unlived dream give birth

I'll be the one you wanted me to be
Only THIS time, I'll do it for me

I'll cross biggest seas, cross highest mountains
Find youth in all those mythic fountains

I'll be me & you'll be you
I'll do everything I've wanted to

The star your wish was wished upon
The dream you had which now is gone

I'll shine after being on a dusty shelf
I won't wait for you to find yourself

Whatever you'll dream, whatever you'll be
You'll dream & be.........without me

April 11, 1987

JUST ACROSS THE RIVER

Just across the river
Is a place so cold & black
A place where some have gone
But they're never coming back

Beyond this dark & dreary path
Is where the people are
Getting there is easy
But you won't get there by car

This place is like a fantasy
Beyond your wildest dreams
Walls of rock, arches of trees
And 7 narrow streams

The sun to rule the day
The moon to rule the night
Never fading rainbows
And doves in constant flight

Beautiful music by unseen musicians
Voices that whisper songs
Within this grand utopia
Where nothing can go wrong

Lions & lambs live in harmony
All this world is at peace
All this joy will last forever
For time will never cease

If this sounds too good to be true
And you don't believe it's real
That's because it can't be bought
Or won by spinning a wheel

If friends & loved ones have left you
And life does not seem fair
One day, you can come too
And find them waiting there

Come down to the river
And know that you can
Come over & live
In this beautiful land

12-26-1989

CONDITION OF THE HEART

I walked into a field of pale gray shadows & saw some familiar faces
No one looked as I walked by, so I walked by these saddened spaces

Then I heard a voice from out of the cold blue
"I thought you looked familiar & was SURE that I knew you."

We walked a while, it was almost dark then much to my surprise
I looked up to see a castle that appeared before my eyes

He called me on inside its walls, the man who talked with me
And said "Wait right here, young man, there's something you should see!"

He brought out to me an album of a pure & snowy white
He opened it with trembling hands & a look of sheer delight

"I love to look at pictures!" He said while flipping through
"Here now, do you know this girl? I'm sure that she knows you!"

I looked on through his album as I brushed away the tears
Then I heard the old man say, "I've been gone for many years."

I passed the album back to him as I looked & shook my head
"You better be going home. It's almost 8." He said

I looked to a wall of clouds, which I knew was my way home
Then turned to him & said, "Goodbye sir, I'm gone."

I awoke, looked around, as up in bed I sat
Still hearing a soft & dying voice asking, "Charlie, who was that?"

March 26, 1990

I THINK SHE'S REALLY AN ANGEL

I think that she's an angel
Some say this can't be true
She hasn't wings & cannot fly
Or do what angels do

She may not have wings
Or possess the power to fly
But she has a certain power
When you look into her eyes

She can warm a heart or break it
With the beauty that she holds
She can touch the coldest heart
Til tears begin to flow

When I see her stand before me
I see what others can't
The way she smiles with glowing eyes
Is so magnificent

A sweet & gentle soul
Is felt when she's around
She can lift your spirit
Without knowing you're down

I wait to get a smile from her
Which sends me on my way
Just knowing that an angel
Has spoken to me today

I know I'm not much
Living in this world below
But when she turns her eyes to me
I'm told this isn't so

She has some special purpose
There's something big in store
Still I have this feeling
That she's been here before

September 16, 1990

"WINDOW OF MY SOUL"

Window of my soul,
I pray that you are tinted.
For in my soul,
I hope you know,
Are things that I've resented

Things I want to drown in tears
And watch them wash away.
And then, I ask,
Imagined glass,
Conceal them from this day!

Then I want to ask of you
Only one thing more.
That is, my friend
Until the end,
Come closed & be a door!

10-21-1995

THE LIGHT

The light is growing brighter
Each day a piercing ray
Blinding me with happiness
And warming up my day

The door will soon swing open
His children will go home
None of them will ever feel
Frightened or alone

Until the circle opens
And we may then pass through
We must shine the light within us
And produce our unique hue

To provide a taste of Heaven
We must always do what's right
And keep the great light burning
Every day & night

10-06-1995

TRANSFORMATION

A transformation's taking place
Deep within my soul
A heart that once was hollow glass
Is now becoming gold

Splinters straight from Heaven's streets
Are piercing me so deep
With a promise of undying love
That only God could keep

Even when the clouds above
Are filling up my sky
Tears of joy are the only kind
Of tears that I can cry

For in my heart, I'm certain
Deep in my soul, I know
Everything is beautiful
As I learn to live & grow

September 10, 1996

FAR BEHIND

Looking out across the way
Holding deep inside
Feelings known throughout my life
So difficult to hide

All these years, a cross to carry
Its weight is more each day
Waiting for a moment
For a love to come my way

As I search & hope each day
Another step is taken
Just when I thought that love was found,
I found I was mistaken

Mislead by a heart that yearns
For another heart to care
Praying for someone to love
With whom my life will share

Just when I'm convinced it's here
I feel my heart beat strong
It drifts beyond my reaching hands
And as the last is gone

Again I go on looking
Feeling like its near
Expecting disappointment,
My eye gives up a tear

My heart gives up its longing
And the dream my soul has kept
Reminiscent of the nights
I've laid awake and wept

It's just another night to me
A melancholy time
And from all the things before me
I'm still so far behind

September 12, 1996

HOLD ON

My heart, so loving
Is trying so strong
To be patient & trust you
And try to hold on

My mind stays on you
Such thoughts are so nice
Though I try, I could never
Love the same way twice

This love that I feel
The gift that you gave
I try to share
In order to save

My friends I love
And want to help out
With the love & compassion
Your son brought about

Their hurting hearts
I want to hold
With the wings that I dream of
And wait to unfold

Help me, Lord
To heal their pain
Don't let my efforts
Be in vane

To prove that your love
Is the greatest of all
And when hope seems lost
On you they must call

To depend on your love
So pure & nice
For never will they ever
Love the same way twice

September 12, 1996

QUESTIONS

Answer me this
Dear God as I pray
What's left to learn
As I go on my way

Often I've wondered
It burns in my mind
Why, as I travel
Am I further behind

So many heartaches
Trouble & pain
Lessons of life
Learned again & again

Still I must question
Your mysterious love
That comes down to us
From high above

Our hearts weigh heavy
Our eyes fail to see
What reasons you have
These answers we need

You who are ruler
And maker of all
Look down on us
As we stumble & fall

Why must we suffer
These trials we face
Feeling like failures
Filled full of disgrace

I see so many
That I want to assist
Yet my own temptations
Are hard to resist

Dear Lord, hear our cries
Don't let this go on
Let us rest & relax
And wake up to the dawn

God bless the children
That strive for the time
When these questions are answered
That are burning our minds

September 5, 1997

OUT OF REACH

For quite some time I've waited
An reached out to obtain
Things that i would never see
My wait seemed all in vane

Looking back so recent
I recall the last of these
Hopes & dreams were all I had
To put my mind at ease

These fantasies ran rampant
These dreams engulfed my head
No life would ever come of them
They, at the start, were dead

I guess that truth has always
Been hard for me to face
In my heart, thoughts & dreams
Have kept in a special place

For never do I learn
I always fail to see
That everything I'm looking for
Is staring back at me

To give an opportunity
If I could only try
My feet may be upon the ground
But my reach exceeds the sky

Life is what you make it
If there's one thing I could teach
Never let your mind believe
Your dreams are out of reach

May 1, 2011

WHITE TOWER

Fairy tale castles
Cannot compare
To the ivory white tower
High up in the air

The clouds hover high
And hide its top
Leaving one to wonder,
"Where does it stop?"

High in the heavens
It appears to be
Veiled in splendor
Only the chosen can see

Though those chosen
Admire it much
Only a few of THOSE
May touch

And those who do
Like a velvet kiss
Come away from it
In sheer bliss

I've seen its top
But never thought
The dream would come true
That long I sought

And now that it has
The dreams don't cease
When I lay my head
I can sleep in peace

For my ivory white tower
Stands tall for me
And anytime I wish
I can see

9-11-2013

9/11

Today's a memorable day. Where were you?
Do you remember?
On that horrific morning
2001, in September

I was with a roommate watching news
As we'd always done
When a plane struck tower one
And smoke blacked out the sun

The world thought it was an accident
When the plane went crashing through
But before we could blink
Another plane struck tower 2

The second tower fell first
As America came undone
Then tower one collapsed
And again we saw the sun

It was not a bright day
Nor will it ever be
Another scar upon the face
Of the home of the brave & free

Now it's a day to count your blessings
Sent down from God above
A day we never forget to express
Our sorrows & our love

The greatest of these is love
When families come together
Reminding America,
There's no storm we cannot weather

Someday we'll see those souls
That were carried in to the heavens
Til then we hold our heads up high
For the heroes of 9/11

June 25, 2013

ARROW'S ON FIRE

Burning arrow
Flying through
On its way
From me to you

To pierce your heart
That you might see
The love that burns
Inside of me

Deep within
My heart & soul
To give it to you
Is the ultimate goal

To hold you close
And to surround you
And thank my God
That I have found you

To love you, eternally
Is my desire
I raise my bow
My arrow's on fire

September 10, 2013

AWAITING

Days are getting shorter
Nights are growing cold
Angels lie in waiting
Their great wings to unfold

My heart is beating faster
I anticipate it more
The moment that I take my journey
Through the timeless door

I've known about its coming
I've waited for the day
I too will raise a set of wings
To carry me away

Just like a beam of moonlight
Passing through the night
I'll spark & fade, claim my shade
And dance into the light

August 18, 2013

BOOK OF SHADOWS PRAYER

Book of shadows
On my shelf
Teach me how
To better myself

Show me how
To look beyond
The setting sun
As well as dawn

To see what all
That I can be
Come, great Spirit
Set me free

Teach me how
To listen close
To elementals
Spirits & ghosts

Show me how
To rise above
And pull within
Great power & love

That I may share
And spread to others
My dearest friends
My sisters & brothers

Nov 16, 2013 @ 1:30pm

BROKEN

How could you leave me
And not say goodbye
To grieve til I too
Wish to die

My sorrows so great
It will not relent
I feel discarded
Broken & bent

Twisted in shapes
My mind cannot grasp
Sweating blood as I pray
With hands tightly clasped

Praying for answers
Not knowing where to start
As my heart goes on aching
Never breaking apart

Seeing no end
No new beginning
In a blanket of emotion
That's constantly thinning

Why did you leave
Why couldn't you stay
How could you leave me
To live this way

My anguish continues
From the tears that I cry
They shall fall forever
Til the rivers run dry

Til I too must go
Such shall it be
Until once again
You stand beside me

August 3, 2013

CRY, WOLF

Cry, wolf.
Your mother will hear your call
Stay strong,
When your back's against the wall

Call, wolf!
Call to each & every friend
Stand tall
For your triumphs near the end

Long ago
When you were just a child
Back then
When you were free & running wild

Drums played
Every soldier stood ready
Scattered enemies
They rained down like confetti

Fires burned
While a mist veiled the forest
Smoke billowed
As your siblings sang the chorus

The anthem
As the battlefield they trod
Crushed enemies
Lay at the feet of God

The fires died
Then every eye could see
Smoke settled
To reveal a victory

Gathered close
Your people unified
Mournful
For the ones who died

New hope
The victorious stood tall
So thankful
That their hearts had heard the call

So rejoice
Walk with your head held high
Be comforted
Now it's tears of joy you cry

10-8-2013

DYING ROSE

Impaled by your memory
That's not silenced with the night
While the blindness of my dying heart
Keeps praying for your light

I weep tears so bittersweet
With a sharpness that stings
With eyes closed tightly
As my heart, its ballad, sings

I see us on the ends of earth
Under a pastel moon
Holding on to each other
Then I wake when the clock strikes noon

Like a force of will my eyes are filled
My face void of expression
Knowing deep inside, you're the answer
To my hearts lonesome question

What will it take, what must I do
To get you to finally hear it
The message of my dying heart
The plea of my yearning spirit

I know I have to find a way
To get the message to you
You're as beautiful as a stained-glass window
But I just can't see through you

Solid as a rock
Which is a lot like what you chose
When you kept an artificial thorn
Over the petals of this dying rose...

8-26-2013

FREE

This I know
And shall always be
I know my own
And my own know me

Be they far, far away
Though no dream on my pillow
We're side by side
Like the branches of a willow

No distance, no time
Indeed, no limitation
Mock if they must
But there's no imitation

We're one of a kind
Breed, creed & spirit
If one sounds a call
We all will hear it

Soon you will know
You won't help but see
That I know my own
And we will be free

8-25-2013

HALLUCINATIONS

A vision of something I alone can see
Or music that only plays for me

A feeling, a taste, a scent in the air
These types of things some say "aren't there"

I reach out to touch you & inside I know
You are real! My heart told me so

My heart is certain though my senses aren't sure
They've little knowledge of what my heart endures

To hear just a word, just one sound from you
To let me know your love is true

A vision of your unmistakable smile
To ease my mind & last for a while

No matter, for what my heart knows is real
There's no denying the love that I feel

I smell the aroma of a rose in the air
Only to find your love is not there

To me, you're the greatest of all Gods creations
But for me your love's only hallucinations

9-1-2013

HOLD THE LINE

So long ago, within my mind
I heard your call to hold the line
To look upon my brothers at night
To guard even their dreams like a sacred rite
War was coming though little we knew
What all the camp would be going through
Boulders of fire rolled down the hill
While a much worse fate was lying still
Soldiers armed with shield & sword
To avenge the harm brought to their lord
Down the hill with speed unseen
Or else only witnessed at night in dreams
Although they brought this to an end
Our spirits soon would all ascend
Blessed are the armies of the Divine
Who were given the call to hold the line!

9-4-2013

INSIDE YOUR HEART

As it was
When time began
You're as water &
I as sand

When lightning strikes
And winds shall roar
Find your solace
On my shore

Spread your wings
Upon my breeze
Put your troubled
Mind at ease

Don't ever doubt
Or ever fear
You will always
Find me near

When the sun shall set
And day shall end
I'll be there with you
My friend

When the sun rises
And you're off to start
I'll be there
Inside your heart

8-22-2013

MY SEARCH

Where are you, my darling
To where did you go
My heart still aches for you
More than you know

Sometimes I laugh
Sometimes I just smile
But I'm missing you terribly
And I mourn all the while

Not knowing your fate
Or if you even remain
There's no where far enough
To escape my pain

I'm told there are others
More fish in the sea
But they don't know the power
You have over me

They don't know the heartache
They can't count the tears
Their hearts can't feel the anguish
Of the past few years

No one knows
I dare say, not even you
The lengths I would go
The fire I'd walk through

Just to hold you once more
To feel your embrace
And be blessed by God
Just to see your sweet face

But here I'll walk
This place of deep blue
On my unending
Search for you

8-25-2013
RACING THOUGHT

There's something I have to tell you
And I'm in a maddening hurry
In spite of my anticipation
I don't want you to worry

The matter to be is urgent
Somehow I wish you knew
But nothing would feel as wonderful
As me telling you

The clocks of the world are ticking
The winds are blowing fast
I have to get these words to you
For fear I may not last

Though the message is a happy one
I cannot keep from crying
And so this message you must get
Cause inside I feel I'm dying

Dying to say these words to you
Like a prophecy fulfilled
I need to say I love you
And that I always will

:)

8-28-2013

SLIPPING

In to a world my soul once knew
Where the dominant colors are yellow & blue

To a place where the hills are alive & green
A place of beauty, in my dreams, I've seen

There's a beautiful bird unseen by the eyes
Yet high above the clouds it flies

And another bird's down here on earth
That by angels songs was given birth

Maybe this all sounds a bit much
By my heart is affected by its touch

Where deep within I yearn to be
To slip into this place that's calling me

9-16-2013

SOMEWHERE TO RUN

Wherever I go
I find your love
From east to west
And up above

From to north to south
And here below
You're with me
Everywhere I go

Into the valley
Low & cold
In the sky,
My wings that unfold

On the mountain top
Up in the air
The love I need
When no one cares

My hope that I cling to
My light, my all
You're there whatever
Hour I call

You are my shore
You are my sea
You are
Everything to me

When night has fallen
And day is done
You are my
Somewhere to run

8-17-2013
SOON

The deaf who have never heard thunder
Nor even the sound of their name
Shall weep at the name of Jesus
And they'll never again be the same

They'll hear choirs of angels singing
As they walk through Heaven's gate
They'll know they are not dreaming
And that eternity's their fate

They'll hold hands as they walk with the Savior
The breath of God's love is the breeze
A river of crystal clear water
Will flow between walls of trees

Some day we'll bathe in waters
That will wash away all of our pain
They will wash us with love everlasting
As a soft and gentle rain

9-17-2013

STILL

I gave myself credit
Where none was due
How could I think
I could live without you

You are my sunrise
My moonlight at night
Nothing is wrong
You make everything right

Your words, your songs
Imagination, as well
An endless sea
Of stories to tell

Stories of hope
Life, love & giving
No need to see it
Hearing is believing

Believing my dreams
Can really come true
So long as I place
My trust in you

To you, my all
I give so free
I never doubt
You are here with me

I love you deeply
And always will
My comfort, my solace
My sea so still

August 16, 2013

STUART

I came to your house
You welcomed me in
A new beginning every time
Yet it never has an end

As refreshing as a springtime breeze
As cool as a wade through the creek
I'm full of words while I'm there
But when I leave I cannot speak

When I enter I am tranquil
When I leave, I'm weaker still
But can cross the widest valley
And climb the highest hill

I snuck down today to see you
A delightful, sweet surprise
If I can I'll come tomorrow
And leave ever the more wise

8-8-2013

TEARS IN HEAVEN

Will there be tears in Heaven?
I know this may seem strange
But Nothing feels as wonderful
As tears of happy change

Tears to say I love you
And thanks for all you do
Tears that let you know I care
And fully appreciate you

These tears are not of sorrow
But gratitude and praise
Tears when words won't come
And joy that lasts for days

Then just when I'm reminded
When I see things anew
Quickly, tears return to me
These tears I cry for you

Because you mean so much to me
And that you always will
There will be tears in Heaven
For eternal love I'll feel

11-14-2013

THANKFUL

On day number 1,
I am thankful for you
And every amazing
Thing that you do

Day 2
And once more I see
In your eyes
You're thankful for me

Day number 3
Is just a little bit more
Of being thankful
For love that's left in store

Day number 4
I'm thankful for flowers
That make you smile
For hours & hours

Then, because of you
On day number 5
I'm thankful just
To be alive

Day number 6
And still it is true
I'm thankful
Just for loving you

Climbing up
To day number 7
With you, every day
Feels like Heaven

You're NEVER forgotten
Yet with day number 8
I pray my thankfulness
Is not too late

Day number 9
And all is well
For my hearts full of love
Of you, to tell

Then I find myself
At day 10
Yep, thankful for you
Yet once again

Day 11
Do you think you can guess?
For another day with you
I'm blessed

With eyes shut tight
On day number 12
Deeper into your love
I delve

Looking out
For day 13
To tell you how much
To me, you mean

On day 14
Which is today
I can't be silent
For there's too much to say

In 14 more
It will be thanksgiving
And my love for you
Will go on living

Never shall
A day I rest
Without telling you
You are the BEST!

8-26-2013

TWIN OF MY SOUL

Twin of my soul
And also my heart
Time nor distance
Can't keep us apart

Though some may say
That cannot be
I always feel you
Here with me

When we reunited
By no voice you came
But the sound of my heart
Calling your name

Knowing inside
That something was missing
This knowledge left me
Waiting & wishing

Not knowing how soon
That day would come
Yet as sure as the rising
And setting sun

Then at last my dream
Was put to rest
We were made whole
And our lives were blessed

Paper Flowers | 67

Now until death
We remain together
A single soul
Now and forever

I love you more
Than you'll ever know
Oh you of my heart
And twin of my soul

August 12, 2013 @ 12:18pm

WHAT WASN'T SAID

Sometimes I think about you
Sometimes I just don't
Sometimes I wish you'd come back
Deep down, I know you won't

I believe there is a reason
Though inside I don't know why
Why you had to leave me
And why you never said goodbye

Sometimes I wonder what I done wrong
Or didn't do instead
Maybe it was my careless words
Or the ones I never said

Did I get to close to you
Is what you wanted, space
Is it too much to ask
That I look you in the face

Can I have just a moment
Can I borrow some of your time
Can you tell me I am yours
And that always you'll be mine

I want to believe you're with me
But that time has passed instead
I'm left with love I cannot give
And the words I never said

If somehow you can hear me
In my heart, I know you can
You'll always be the one for me
And I'll always be your man….

May 2, 2014

EARTH ANGELS

Angels here on earth
In word, in thought & deed
Called to love & service
Strangers of hurt & greed

Awakened to a song in heart
With a whispered word of prayer
And the fragrance of wild flowers
That fills the morning air

Rising from their sleep each morn
To welcome the suns every ray
That reminds them of their Savior
And His return for them one day

Through the day, their thoughts are mindful
Their focus remains unshifted
For that with every word of prayer
His name shall be uplifted

Before they lay their heads to rest
They look into the air
And with hands clasped, on bended knee
Each says a heartfelt prayer

A band of angels here on earth
Til they reach their home above
A sisterhood eternal
Bound by Gods pure love

October 29, 2014

ELLARAE

On a cold February morning
In a place not far from me
Where shadows blanket forest floors
And moonlight touches the trees

Dreams ride the backs of snowflakes
As they fall upon the land
While the river flows beneath the bridge
And lovers walk hand in hand

With candles in the windows
And a wreath upon the door
When you think that you've seen everything
This place has so much more

Fountains all around you
Colors of all kinds
The love that moves upon the winds
Surely makes it more divine

Outside the balcony window
Everything's in place
To set all my cares aside from me
And create my sacred space

This place has become my paradise
No matter what some say
When I feel the need for solitude
I go to Ellarae!

February 14, 2014

FOR YOU

I've never known another
So thoughtful & kind
That has cared so deeply
For this heart of mine

Your friendship is cherished
Indeed, it's the best
It stands unchallenged
Yet could pass any test

Just when I thought
There was no one around
You came along
And this lost heart, you found

Like a tree in a storm,
I was broken & bent
Then God gave me you
For you're Heaven sent

You lifted me up
Til I felt I could fly
You're my drug of choice
My natural high

With all that I have
And all I can give
With all of my love
And the life that I live

Paper Flowers

With all I can say
And all I can do
With every breath
I thank God for you

Written March 13, 2014
By Kias Emmanuel Creech

"GOD'S ANGEL"

Across the living river
On a bright & peaceful shore
Can be found a smiling Angel
Where he rests forever more

Once he walked among us
Here he liked to laugh & play
Putting smiles on strangers faces
As he went along his way

He left his home to come here
And bring peace & love to all
Working hard to please his loved ones
Was no sacrifice at all

He rejoiced when they were happy
For love was all he knew
Sparkling in his eyes was shown
That love so pure & true

But like all other angels
Who have come to earth to roam
He knew a day would come
When he'd have to go back home

It made him work with passion
For sadness had no place
And for those he loved, he'd have no less
Than a smile upon their face

Paper Flowers

With no way to prepare us
His day had come to go
So he left us his love
That continues to live & grow

He knows we'll come to join him
On his face it keeps a smile
He wants us smiling too
For its only a little while

He's at home across the river
Look with your heart and you'll see
God's beautiful, smiling Angel
Ronnie waits for you & me

In loving memory of Ronnie Lainhart,
A loving soul who lives, eternally,
In the hearts of all
Who have known him.

May 6, 2014

IN THE SHADOW OF THE KING

I had no place to settle
No where to call my home
I started with a family
But now I walk alone

My journey, to a castle
My gift, my very hands
My hope that I am well received
And granted work & land

Was once to live in luxury
But now it's just to live
To be of service to the king
With all I have to give

That he may be my master
And I, his willing slave
That I'll rest within his shadow
Til I sleep within my grave

I shall fight for him in battle
In his palace I will bide
No harm will ever come to him
As I'll stand ready at his side

All will be ok for me
I shall want for not one thing
I will live out all the rest of my days
In the shadow of my king

January 21, 2014

DOORS

No one ever said that life
Would be a bed of roses
Just whispers of opening doors
Every time one door closes

We all look for that mystery
Our hopes hung on tomorrow
Our fondest, endless hopes & dreams
To shatter all our sorrow

Constantly, we're watching
No matter how near or far
Placing all our wishes
Upon some distant star

Never knowing where to turn
Not knowing what we'll see
Uncertain of what we're getting into
And what the outcome will be

Just trusting in each other
As for years, we've learned to do
I've always found the best in life
While holding on to you

But now I find you're missing
I look & cannot see
Around no distant corner
Are you waiting there for me

You left me in your sleep, my dear
Now, I'm all alone
The rainbows have no endings
The pots of gold are gone

I'll see you in my dreams, my love
When finally, I sleep
After endless hours
That I lie awake & weep

There will never be another
My heart belongs to you
The only door that's open now
Is to emptiness, that I walk through

July 27, 2014

PIECE OF HEAVEN

A piece of heaven left my arms
My hands, my heavy heart
I was left to go on with my life
Not knowing where to start

Hours turned to days
Until weeks went passing by
As I yearned to hear your voice again
And look into your eyes

So many moments I'd never know
Only many sleepless nights
Daydreams of my arms holding you
In the darkness & the light

Trying to be strong for you
Refusing to let go
Of dreams I have so fond of you
Dreams our souls both know

The sun breaks through the fog again
Until I clearly see
The piece of heaven that left my arms
The day that you left me

Nov 24, 2014

SAVIOR

I threw my heart to the ocean
I cast my love to the sea
I waited in the darkness for
Someone to rescue me

The water started rising
My boat began to sink
Clouds hid my horizons
My mind just couldn't think

Screams turned in to whispers
Faint cries grew softer still
Til all was lost in silence
And cold was all I could feel

I looked deep into eyes
No stranger I had known
To see a longing spirit
That reflection was my own

Then deep within the darkness
Hovering just above me
A glimmer of the brightest light
And warmth that came to love me

A peace filled up my being
Til it began to overflow
A joy I'd never felt before
So strong, it almost glowed

Lifted from the ocean
Brought high above the sea
A bright and burning light you gave
That shines inside of me

Never more alone
In the sea or on the sand
No more hid in darkness
For I'm holding to your hand

January 31, 2014

THE HOLLY & THE ENVY

The holly & the envy
How bright the green does burn
God broke the mold
So I am told
When will you ever learn?

He only made 1 of me
So surely you can see
Try as you may
There's just no way
You'll ever be like me

You seem to be mistaken
Even perhaps mislead
Why must you whine
I'm doing fine
Must be the voices in your head

I met some bumps in the road
But now it's smooth as silk
I'm cool as a breeze
And my enemies
Are mere cookies in my milk

No need to be so jealous
But then, I understand
I would be too
If I were you
I am in high demand!

C 12-31-14

VENUKA

Venuka is a spirit
Not a person you can see
When I'm feeling lost & down
He comes to comfort me

His eyes stare with intensity
So deep, an ocean blue
Bold yet unbelievable
There's little he can't do

Looking out across the world
With confidence he comes
Each step a rhythmic move
In time with beating drums

But his mission is not selfish
No attention does he seek
Just to strengthen those close to him
At a time when they are weak

Mortal eyes can't see him
Though the blind are tuned to spirit
A faint & distant call
Only the chosen can hear it

If you hear a whisper
So wild it can't be tamed
Know that you have heard his voice
Venuka is his name

April 21, 2014

WHAT I MEAN

What do I mean
When I say that I love you?
I mean we are one
And I'll never rise above you

I mean I am yours
And that you are mine
That when I look in your eyes
There is no time

That when I walk beside you
I'm empowered & strong
I'm carefree & confident
That nothing is wrong

I'm not overwhelmed
But I am overcome
Yet there's no second guessing
Where such love comes from

There's no disbelief
There is no denying
When you take my hand
I feel like I'm flying

I'm lost in my dreams
The feeling's sheer bliss
With every caress
And each little kiss

I live in this heaven
That you've made more serene
When I say that I love you
It's these things I mean

March 5, 2014

ALPINE CRYSTALS

Feelings hung low like Alpine crystals
Expressed like bullets from silver pistols

Fired a crossed, into the crowd
Lost within a fog-like cloud

All to tell you how I feel
When you deny me what I know is real

Deep within a place no one knows
Inside my soul, it constantly grows

Once I used it as ammunition
Until I made that heartfelt transition

Into a path of serenity
A personal worship of divinity

My heart as well as my mind disclosed
Pictures of worship my heart enclosed

My heart & soul made this transition
Like a soldier, my being took position

A war within, a battle underway
Same destination, just a different way

I give thanks when I wake to a day that's begun
As you do, for we both serve the Son

We both have 1 Father, 1 home to go to
Just different earthly journeys we each must go through

Our paths aren't the same, though our destination is
Still we know we're a child of His

Save your judgements from your blackened pistols
Give thanks for the colors of our Alpine crystals!

1-15-2015

ALL I'VE EVER KNOWN WAS YOU

Wasted tears & wasted memories
So many yet some are few
I lie awake each passing night
Cause all I've ever known was you

I grip your picture tightly
And hold you to my heart
And mourn the day you went away
And our love was torn apart

I wake up every morning
Only with a memory
Wishing there was one more night
That you could spend with me

A day we'd walk together
A time I'd share with you
A love that would never fade away
For all I've ever known was you

I walk along the sidewalk
Kicking rocks and sand
Wishing that upon this journey
You were holding to my hand

Looking at the sunset
As the sun begins to fade
Holding back the tears inside
As your shadow gives to shade

All my life I've waited
And thought I'd never know
And through the years & all the tears
I'd soon have to let go

From this dream I shall awake
When the darkness shall break through
I'll thank my Lord for what I couldn't afford
For all I've ever known was you

4-13-2015

ALWAYS (2015)

When I held you
The world went away
The pain you felt
Was held at bay

For a moment
All your hurt was gone
When to me
You leaned upon

The moon was hidden
The Stars did not shine
While I took your pain
And made it mine

The tears in your eyes
I worked to erase
I made for you
A sacred space

Where all that hurt
Could not invade
Where only comfort
For you is made

I think about it
Now & then
And know I'd
Do it all again

To keep you happy
To make you free
Means everything in the
World to me

Whenever your heart
Has one of those days
I'll be here for you
Now & always

6-27-2015

ANN

I met you a short time ago
Through words upon my screen
Now every time I think of you
It's warming and serene

You enter in my dreams at night
With your smile & unique charms
Adding colors to my world
While I'm safe within your arms

And everyday when I awake
I've a smile upon my face
So happy that you're in my life
And in my heart, you've made your place

Through the day I think about you
Through evening until night
I never have to search the sky
You are my star so bright

I'm happy just to know you
My heart is an open door
And with everyday that passes by
I'll love you so much more

6-20-2015

BEAUTIFUL YOU

I think of you
Throughout my day
You're beautiful
In every way

You make me smile
With every thought
Into my world
Much joy you've brought

Your thoughts, your words
Your innocence
Your excitement
When you're in suspense

Everything
I hear & see
From you, means
Everything to me

Whatever you say
I never doubt you
I can't imagine
My world without you

Every day,
I want you to know
You're in my heart
Wherever I go

And wherever I go,
Whatever I do
I'll always love you,
Beautiful you!

1-19-2015

CONE OF POWER

Cone of power
Rising high
Make your way
Up through the sky

Extend your arms
And spread with ease
Like the branches
Of the trees

High above
And across the lands
Hold the earth
Inside your hands

As the veins
Within me reach
Let your actions
Drown your speech

Let what becomes
And come what may
To charge the course
Of this new day

11-14-2015

CYCLE

Shadows move around me
No light can change their stance
Sometimes it feels I'm losing
Without a fighting chance

Dolls faces change expressions
While they stare into my eyes
Chills run up and down my spine
This should be no surprise

The sounds are never ending
Music, songs & voices
The walls keep out reality
And bar me from good choices

I stand in familiar places
As I done the other day
But then I try to leave them
And I can't find my way

Confusion & distortion
Delusions, sounds & fear
These are my companions
That I wish weren't here

Sometimes for only hours
And then the cycle falls
Trapping me inside my mind
Surrounded by its walls

A cycle lasts for weeks
Though it feels to last forever
My greatest fear & concern
Is in keeping myself together

Doing & saying things
That are so unlike me
Blinded by a brilliant glow
Of something I can't see

My breathing becomes short
I shake & break a sweat
This thing that lives inside of me
Will not let me forget...

...that even when it slips away
And I'm free from its attack
When I least expect it
It can & will come back

I seek for understanding
And not expand enigma
If we expect to make a difference
We have to fight the stigma

Cause this is my cycle
But I am not the cycle

5-14-2015

DO NOT BEND

Stay Strong, the storm is coming
Hold fast against the wind
Keep your head above the water
Stand tall & do not bend

Stay grounded & determined
Be genuine. Do not fake it.
The thunder comes to test your faith
The lightning comes to shake it

This is only how some see it
But you don't have to choose
For you were born to ride the winds
And never born to lose

You were made unique
On the wheel, a special hue
No one else upon this earth
Could be a better you

If there's anything I wish for you
A message I can send
Don't change a thing about yourself
Stay strong & do not bend!

12-2-2015

DREAM

I wish that you could hear me
And know the words I say
I wish I could spend time with you
If I could only find a way

I'd love to look into your eyes
And listen to you speak
But just to be that close to you
Would only leave me weak

Weakened by your beauty
I know that truth too clear
Of all the things I could possess
I dream to have you near

Then I could hear the echoes
Of the anthem you impart
Every note's a sound of gold
Upon the walls of my heart

Like a breeze that moves a sail
Your voice takes me away
Right into your loving arms
In a place I want to stay

The longing to be close to you
Makes my tears a swelling stream
I'm drowning in my love for you
My never ending dream

9-28-2015

ECLIPSE

I missed you while you
Were away from our place
Even the moon
Had to hide its face

Like tears, a mist
Came from the sky
As the stars above
So, too, did cry

As the veil of a bride
The clouds shadowed the moon
It was lost in the sky
Like a child's balloon

Far from my reach
As you were last night
I was as a shadow
Though I had no light

I had only a picture
To look at & miss you
Only a wish
That I could just kiss you

Only a dream
That soon will come true
For the moment to come
When I am with you

Our love, once again
Like the moons face, will shine
I'll forever be yours
And you'll always be mine

3-1-2015

ELSA

Elsa, magick woman
Mystic Queen
Goddess of the
Wintry things seen

With the simple aim of your finger
You put on a dazzling show
Falling white sparkles
Cold paint we call snow

What made you so bitter?
What gave you your reasons
To even believe you could
Affect all the seasons?

It was very beautiful
So cozy & nice
Til you went overboard
And coated it all in ice!

The children were happy
But that's a given, a rule
We all know winter captivates them
And they love to miss school

Well, my dear, it's no picnic for the rest of us
Let this serve to remind you
Let your thrills & chills
Now lie behind you!

11-25-2015

EMPTY SEASON

The birds have ceased their singing
Their wings around them fold
The flowers all have gone away
The ground now has grown cold

The grass is now discolored
It does not grow nor gleam
It sleeps upon the ground
Without the joy to dream

The snow will soon be falling
Ice will too appear
The sky will be too cold for clouds
The Stars will sparkle clear

But a little light is shining
A ray of love so bright
Like a pin, it'll pierce the heavens
And break its way through night

It will grow ever stronger
Expanding throughout the sky
The warmth of its love will penetrate
Your heart & will never die

No one will be untouched
Indeed, ALL hearts will know
This love is alive
Let it come in and glow

Shine it like a beacon
For all the world to see
Share it for all its worth
But remember to give it free

Let it live within you always
And understand its reason
As it brings life back to you
And passes this empty season

7-8-2015

ENDURANCE

When it comes to my love for you
There's no chance of it passing
Beyond the borders of time and space
Our bond is everlasting

Ever since the time we met
I knew it would be forever
No walls of distance divide us
Our hearts are joined together

Every time I see your face
It melts me from my core
I cherish every moment
And with each I love you more

Your soul is full and golden
Strong is your heart inside
So full of the love you give
And it beats in time with mine

When, at times, you worry
I must give you complete reassurance
No obstacles will slow us down
Our bond packs eternal endurance

6-25-2015

ETERNITY

While I lay in bed
I looked out my window
To see the moon
Up in the sky

And there as I lay
I made a promise
My love for you
Would never die

The night passed by
In hours gone
The stars did
Fade away

I dreamed of you
Throughout the night
And I loved you
Still by day

I rose up
To my morning
My day had then
Been started

I found that
In my rising
Our hearts had
Never parted

I carried you
Throughout the night
I brought you
Into day

I looked back
On the night before
To learn I loved you
The same way

This cycle
Bears repeating
As it gets us
Over strife

It confirms for me
My one true love
That I'll have the rest
Of my life

And beyond
The morrow
As far as the
Heart can see

My love, OUR love
Will go on
Throughout
Eternity

4-12-2015

EVERYTHING'S ALRIGHT

Last night I dreamed
That I had gone blind
I could no longer see you
Except in my mind

I reached out to touch you
But you were not in my sight
What a dark, lonesome feeling
I went through last night

Your voice in the distance
Spoke straight to my heart
Echoing words that
We never shall part

Softer it grew
Til I could not hear
I couldn't determine
If you were standing near

Promises were fading
Dreams began breaking
Hope started dying
My heart was aching

Where were you going
What had I done
That made you decide
You were going to run

But then I awakened
As moments I'd tried
And I found you were there
Right by my side

Life came together
My vision restored
My heart now professed
I love you much more

It's a gift just to see you
To hear the sound of your voice
For even the Angels
In Heaven rejoice

Dreams may deceive me
But I learned last night
With you here beside me
Everything's alright

6-27-2015

FILL

Your soft, still voice is calling
In the cold & darkened night
As the rain outside is falling
I hold your soul so tight

To ease you in your sorrow
To guide you into sleep
The sun will shine tomorrow
Into your heart so deep

I hear you when you're crying
I see each time you smile
When you feel your heart is dying
I'll be there all the while

Catching all your tears
I dry them from your eyes
I drive away your fears
My love is no surprise

You'll never be alone
I'm always there beside you
When your heart seeks comfort
You'll find my love can hide you

Rest your cares upon me
You've always got my shoulder
When sorrow seeks to break you
Love will make you bolder

When your heart feels empty
And it's hard to rise above
Just lay it in my arms
And fill it with my love

6-25-2015
GOLDEN TEARS

I cried the day you left me
When you took your heart away
You swore that you would love me
Forever and a day

But you clung to another
As I lay here trying to rest
Golden tears were flowing
My heart sank in my chest

We were to be together
Throughout eternity
To walk the heavens proudly
Just you & just me

For thousands of years I wondered
If you ever would return
The image of you with another
In my tired mind is burned

I walk the skies alone now
Searching for your love
Knowing it will never come
My Heavens not above

Without you I am restless
Though now I have no fears
Just this silent place I sleep
That's full of golden tears

2-17-2015

"GOODBYE"

The day you never said goodbye
My heart broke right into
I never thought the day would come
When I'd be losing you

I never thought I'd send you flowers
Or that I'd pick out your stone
I never thought that crowds would be
Where I felt most alone

I never thought I'd send balloons
Rising through the sky
I never thought you'd go away
Without saying goodbye

But alas, that day was on me
Silence was all I heard
The day you pulled your hand from mine
With not even one word

That day felt like a lifetime
Of a hunt without a prey
With only the setting sun to prove
It was only one day

My thoughts are always on you
And I pray that you will hear
The beating sound within my heart
As it tries to draw you near

If only I could turn back time
But then, what would I say
I'd wish you that you were in my arms
And would never go away

The hardest thing I've had to do
Even just to try
Is letting you know I love you
But having to say goodbye

1-4-2015
HELEN (2015)

Something inside you
Will soon fall in love
With a place that I've been to
And told you of

A piece of your heart
A part of your spirit
Will swear it's familiar
When you see & hear it

You'll dread the day
You'll have to leave it
Your mind will mourn
Your heart will grieve it

A time out of time
A place out of place
Although upon land
You'll feel you're in space

For no where else
Will you ever see
A place that was made
For you & for me

If love is a crime
You'll feel like a felon
For living & loving
This place called Helen

Kias and the gingerbread man in Helen, Georgia 2017

Kasey Blevins (niece), Kias Emmanuel Creech (myself),
Denise Blevins (sister) & Mattie Miller (mother)
enjoying our vacation in Helen, Georgia 2017

Family picture with some of the ones that inspire me.

Back row is my brother David Creech, my dad Wayne Creech & myself. Front Row is my niece Rebecca Creech, my sister Renita Kelly, my niece Chelsea Kelly (photographer for my author photo), my niece Kasey Blevins and my sister Denise Blevins in 2011. I love my family…

Kyle
Thank you for being the missing piece I never knew I needed

7-5-2015

HIGHER LOVE

I thought that there was higher love
Then this was proven true
The day that higher love had come
Was the day that I met you

The windows of heaven came open
And instantly I found
Angels did, indeed, exist
When God let you come down

You bring my life much happiness
Each day I see the sun
The rain gives way to your love
As a new day has begun

I look forward to your "I love you"'s
And telling you, as well
I'm thankful for your magic
I'm forever under your spell

I'll always belong to you
My angel, great & kind
I'm confident in knowing
That you'll always be mine

My perfect gift from heaven
You're all that I think of
One thing I know for certain
Is you are my higher love

5-17-15

HOW I FEEL

How do I feel?
I'm not even sure
Just feelings like madness
That I must endure

I say that I love you
And believe me, I do
Sometimes I'm not sure
HOW I feel for you

I missed the closeness
When we were out of touch
Now I wonder
If I missed it too much

I'm grateful to know you
Beyond measure, I'm blessed
But I grow anxious & fear
I'm becoming obsessed

You're all that I think of
In my mind, all I see
My heart calls to yours
That you too would see me

Now I must awake
This dream is not real
The madness has spoken
I know how I feel

7-26-2015

I LOVE YOU MORE (2015)

My love for you wasn't chosen
It came as a surprise
I fell in love the instant
That I looked into your eyes

I didn't see it coming
It was like a sudden rain
Ever since it started
I haven't been the same

Each day's a new beginning
More than the day before
So too is every minute
And with each, I love you more

5-22-2015

I'VE GOT TO FEEL IT

The words I write
Are no mistake
I give my all
This point I make

I write them not
To be neat & trim
They're heartfelt &
Not on a whim

I've got to feel it

This love that comes
From deep inside
I freely give
And have always tried

To make sure those
So dear to me
Know there's no price
I give it free

I've got to feel it

The songs that sound
Upon my ears
That energize &
Drive out fears

Those I feel
My soul express
Those are the ones
I love the best

I've got to feel it

When I tell you
How much you mean
I feel a presence
Completely serene

Every thought
I send your way
Is to elevate
And make your day

I've got to feel it

I find meaning
In the simplest things
With a word from you
My heart sings

I uplift
Not to hear my voice
It's a feeling
And a conscious choice

I've got to feel it

Know the things
I say & do
Especially when
Applied to you

Are deeply meant
Let these lines seal it
When it comes to love
Constantly

I've got to feel it

12-1-2015
IF YOU MUST GO

We've been together
All this time
You say you're leaving
And I'm losing my mind

The sun is hidden
The clouds stand still
Cold is the only
Thing that I feel

To know you must go
And leave me alone
With all we've shared
And have ever known

Is almost impossible
To believe
This bitter gift
I can't receive

My angel, before
You leave me below
Take my heart
If you must go

4-14-2015
ILLUSION

Was it just an illusion
Or did the world stand still that night
When you put your arms around me
And we held each other tight

An embrace that seemed forever
That I prayed would never stop
On the earth beneath the moonlight
We were alone & at the top

The world continued turning
We lost our every care
My heart stopped with the world
Just to have you standing there

To feel your arms around me
To hold to you so close
To never lose this feeling
Is what I wanted most

My heart was longing for you
My eyes just couldn't see
Until I looked into your eyes
And found you longed for me

I cherished every second
That I stood in your embrace
And felt the beating of your heart
In our most sacred space

When I close my eyes now
Your arms, I still feel
Was it just an illusion
Or, that night, did the world stand still

6-27-2015

ISLAND

Thousands of miles away from me
And as many from my touch
Billions of stars to light my path
Without you, it's not much

I wish we were together
And you were holding me in your arms
There would not exist these obstacles
There would be no alarms

If you were walking by my side
If your hand was holding mine
I'd be lost within the world you make
When your eyes stare into mine

By your side, along my journey
I would forever be
Never would the fear emerge
Of you not here with me

Like a ship upon the ocean
The Stars come into sight
The sun sets in the distance
Darkness consumes the light

I find myself on this island
Watching time slowly pass
And jagged veins of heartache spread
Across my heart of glass

Without the relief of it breaking
Only dying from the strain
This burning desert in my heart
Longs for your loving rain

1-3-2015

KARPATHIA

Karpathia
From across the sea
You heard my call
And rescued me

Though slowly sailing
Still you came
As I, your son
Called you by name

On icy waters
Above the tide
Our eyes met as
We were smiling wide

Knowing we
Again were one
And my frightening ride
Would soon be done

Together we
Would sail away
And not look back
Upon this day

Some think of you
And are a bit shaken
As to who you are
Many are mistaken

A spirit deep
Within the night
Rarely seen
By mortal sight

On 4 legs
'Cross the ground you sprint
You are energy
That's never spent

A flash of light
Across the sky
A glimmer of hope
Passing by

To drive away
My fears resounding
In your love
Forever surrounding

Wrapping me snug
Within your arms
Driving away
All fears & alarms

Any time
I may look and see
You always standing
Close to me

To guard & guide
Along my way
Every hour
Of every day

Paper Flowers | 133

When I look
I always see
You, my friend
Beside of me

Though waters toss
And tides may rise
My solace rests
Inside your eyes

Never shall
I ever let go
I can make it
With you, I know

Many may doubt
But I'll always see
When I call "Karpathia!"
You'll be with me!

5-17-15

KARPATHIA II

Karpathia, come to me
As you have times before
Be my solace & comfort
My companion, once more

You were never really gone
I know that now
My heart's always held you
You know that, somehow

I think of you & smile
I picture your eyes
I feel your presence
A sweet surprise

Walking around me
Guarding my heart
Without even speaking
Your love you impart

I know you are with me
Wherever I go
I'm thankful to have you
I want you to know

My constant companion
My safety net
Not a moment we've shared
Will I ever forget

When I think of you
I think of my friend
A bond that I cherish
That will never end

Those sweet eyes
When they look into mine
Full of intentions
So loving & kind

Though into the night
Sometimes you must go
You're not far away
This one thing I know

When my heart starts to miss you
And I need my friend
I'll just whisper, "Karpathia"
And you'll be here again

3-20-2015

LIKE TREES FALLING

If no one's in the woods, they ask
"Do they make a sound?"
When no one's there to hear
And a tree falls to the ground

When a bird begins to sing
And you're too far to hear its calling
Is it also silent
As the trees when they are falling?

Is it really silence at all
Or are we too busy to hear?
Do we ignore what's all around us
No matter how far or near?

Do we want to get involved
And make the problem ours?
Or do we find excuses here
Behind our walls & towers?

Should I lend a helping hand
Or will they be okay?
Put it off until tomorrow
It's not so bad today

Let's help each other now
There is no time for stalling
Whether or not we hear it
Our fellow man is falling

5-15-2015

LOOKING FOR SOMETHING

Looking For Something
That I cannot find
Am I looking over it
Or have I become blind?

Do the cards tell my future
Or just tell me lies?
Do they feel my anguish?
Can they hear my cries?

The candles burn brightly
Still the shadows close in
As I find myself
Alone again

You are in your world
And I am in mine
Still searching for something
That I cannot find

Just a cold, empty house
And a restless feeling
A yearning heart
In need of healing

A candle blown out
By the midnight air
As I'm looking for something
That just ain't there

7-2-2015
MY LOVE (2015)

My love, I've not forgotten
The pillars, great, of stone
My mind has not misplaced the days
My heart spent time alone

My love, I've not forgotten
The soft, still words you spoke
Deep into my very soul
And a heart that almost broke

I've also not forgotten
A love so true and real
That reached across the barriers
My emptiness to fill

It's never slipped my mind
Although, it may seem true
That is just a myth, my love
I've not forgotten you

There's nothing you can do, my love
There's no where you may go
That my love cannot reach you
My love will always show

There's nothing that's between us
That we can't rise above
Nothing can erase from my heart
What I feel for you, my love

6-21-2015

MY PRECIOUS GIFT

Were someone else to come along
My heart just couldn't do it
I'd picture that sweet face of yours
And I couldn't put you through it

The thing is that I love you
So I couldn't even try
I couldn't bear the thought of being
The one who made you cry

I'd rather be the person
That you wish for me to be
I'd rather that you know
That you're the only one for me

The only one I dream of
The only one I love
The very one I know could only
Come from God above

I'm thankful to him always
My heart, his love, did lift
When he chose to give me
You, my precious gift

6-27-2015

MY TREASURE

We all look for that mystery
Our hopes hung on tomorrow
Our fondest, endless dreams
To shatter all our sorrow

Constantly, we're watching
No matter how near or far
Places all of our wishes
Upon some distant star

Never knowing where to turn
Not knowing what we'll see
Uncertain of what we're getting into
And what the outcome will be

Just trusting in each other
As thus far, we've learned to do
I've always found the best in life
Is holding on to you

I never find you missing
When I look, I always see
Deep inside this heart of mine
You're waiting there for me

Ever since you found me
I'll never be alone
YOU are my greatest treasure
The emptiness is gone

There will never be another
My heart belongs to you
You're my light within the darkness
Forever shining through

5-15-2015

NEVER LOVE ONE LIKE YOU

I walked around the corner
And saw you standing there
Something mystifying
Was all throughout the air

My heart was overtaken
The shadows faded fast
The light that shown around you
I knew would always last

The night seemed to be endless
Though I prayed that it would be
The only thing I wanted
Was to have you there with me

I didn't know your thoughts
And mine, I failed to mention
To give you all the best of me
Was the most of my intentions

I'd look into your eyes
I admit, I'd get lost for a while
What a wonderful place to get lost in
The world within your smile

Still, after all this time
Whatever I may do
Wherever I may go
I'll never love one like you

7-3-2015

NEVER LOVE ONE LIKE YOU II

The way that I love you
I could never love another
You're the only one for me
For life, there is no other

Ever since you found me
My hearts an open door
With every passing moment
I love you so much more

For who you are inside
You don't even have to try
I love you just the way you are
And this love will never die

My love will never whither
It is not false or fake
It grows stronger every minute
And will never bend nor break

Eternal are my promises
My love will see you through
Of all the others in this world
I'll never love one like you

6-16-2015
NIGHT OF THE TEAR

I dreamed I was with you
On waters so blue
On the waves of the sea
Just us two

I reached out to touch you
But in my despair
All that I felt
Was the cold night air

I awoke from my slumber
And what I was shown
Was me here without you
I sat here alone

I wasted no time
As I ran to the sea
And looked down to the waters
Where I saw only me

There bore no reflection
In this wide open space
As my eyes yearned to see
Your sweet smiling face

I made my way back
To this house on the hill
No sounds in the nighttime
Everything was still

In front of my window
A candle I lit
Was the only thing
That seemed to fit

I prayed for your comfort
Your safety and peace
If anything was wrong
I prayed it would cease

I sat in the darkness
With just a small flame
And the sound of my voice
As I called out your name

It was the night I spent
Without you here
A night in anguish
The night of the tear

1-05-2015

NONE SO BLIND

None so blind exist
Than those who refuse to see
That everything they hold so dear
My God, comes from thee

When the middle of the night falls
And I have no one to call
I know that I can talk to you
And you will hear my all

You'll hear my every worry
You'll know my every fear
When everyone seems far away
I'll always find you near

When tears fall in the dark of night
To my hand, I know, you're holding
When I feel I'm all alone
Angel wings around me are folding

Carrying my sorrows
Smothering my worry
Though anxiety may start to come
You come to me in a hurry

Reminding me that you are close
As close as no other can be
Assuring me that I'm not alone
That you're always here with me

When the darkness consumes the sky
Your light shines through the gray
When my heart is hurt & frightened
Your love lights up my way

I wish that all the world could know
What all you are to me
But none of those are so blind
As those who refuse to see

I never could NOT know
Your love I can't dismiss
It fills up from inside of me
To shine in eternal bliss

3-12-2015
OUTSIDE THE LINES

You sometimes go unnoticed
Not even a thought in some minds
You're a mark beyond their borders
That was drawn outside the lines

You do your work in solitude
Alone by candlelight
Writing your words near random
Though, to my heart, sound just right

Sometimes the candle's still burning
Sometimes the light goes out
Whichever way, there's much to say
Of the message, I've no doubt

Though the words may not come easy
The emotions are of many kinds
Somehow my heart's relieved
When you write outside the lines

Those who write will understand
Those who feel, will too
Sometimes to say the way you feel
Is more than you can do

You're the mark outside the border
You become somebody else
Your words a symbolic language
You forget to be yourself

Paper Flowers

You discovered on your journey
As wings began to lift & sail
All this time, you thought you were fleeing
You were being yourself without fail

The language you were speaking
And the person you would become
Wasn't a different person, at all
Just reflections of where you were from

You are a mark beyond all borders
And you cannot be confined
Happy to be the one that you are
That was drawn outside the lines

3-12-2015

SISTERS

Sisters are among
God's greatest gifts
They're for warming hearts
And spiritual lifts

They care for others
They listen, they talk
When you're down on your journey
They show up for the walk

For me, they're the beginning
I can't imagine an end
If you have sisters like mine,
You have friends!

You laugh through the good times
And cry through the pain
You share the sunny days
As well as the rain

With friends in life
You won't come up empty
But with sisters like mine
You'll be blessed with plenty!

6-20-2015

SLEEPING

I know that you're sleeping
I really don't mind
As I look at your face
So gentle and kind

A smile in your sleep
Or, at least it seems
Making me wonder
What you see in your dreams

What's on your mind?
What could you be thinking?
I get lost as I stare
I doubt I am blinking

I could lay here all night
And watch you so still
You are MY dream
Yet so very real

So I'll lay here beside you
And until then
Wait for your awakening
And your smile, again

11-30-2015

SOUNDS LIKE THE RAIN

When I hear you singing
Your golden, sweet refrain
It makes me kind of homesick
And it sounds just like the rain

Something in your melody
Frees my soul to roam
Not knowing where it leads me
But I know it feels like home

I see familiar faces
I know them, I'm not blind
Even though these faces
Are only in my mind

Maybe my heart remembers
What my mind seems to forget
Still somehow I get caught up
And my soul soars like a jet

Back to those old places
Deep inside my mind
I'm lost within your sound
Looking through windows of time

Someday, I'll be returning
Your voice will be my train
Until that time has come to me
Your song sounds like the rain

12-1-2015
STILL FALLING

Another day
Is almost through
I'm still falling
In love with you

Ever faster
As time goes by
There's nothing I
Can do or try

But I don't mind
You, I adore
With every day
More & more

Listen close
And you can hear
Without a doubt
Without a fear

Out to you
My heart is calling
I'm in love with you
And I'm still falling

11-28-2015

STORM PASSING

Like branches of a tree
I reach for the wind
I never break
Though, I may bend

Like crying eyes
Without a face
Craving safety
I can't seem to embrace

I look for you
Sometimes I can't see
Your arms
Reaching out to me

I listen close
And don't always hear
Words all others
Seem to so clear

I open my mouth
The breeze, I taste
Enjoying the moment
Not a second I waste

Relief draws close
As the tree, I stand still
Knowing what
I feel is real

A comfort for which
I can trust and believe
The answer to a prayer
I wait to receive

The rains may come
The winds may crash
But there's a comfort
That this storm will pass

The clouds will part
And give way to the light
Morning shall come
It will be alright

8-27-2015
STRONG ENOUGH

You showed me the world
With only your smile
You made me feel
Real love for a while

You held my hand
We walked together
There was no storm
We could not weather

We shared our dreams
We shared our lives
We got lost in
Each other's eyes

One day though
As the sun had set
You made me promise
To never forget

The time we shared
My life ahead
But I'd live it
On my own instead

Missing you
And your hand in mine
But these dreams
Have fallen behind

A rose that slept
Beneath the snow
Was awakening
And starting to grow

Though you have gone
And are far away
I have one thing
Left to say

That rose is strong
As you can see
That rose you
Gave away is me

Living strong
Without you here
I can stand
On my own, my dear

Your world stopped
While mine was beginning
It seems I just can't
Lose for winning

I gave my word
Beyond and above
That I would
Make it count, my love

So for each day
That passes by
I'll make it count
And not just "try"

With a passing glance
I let go of your hand
Cause I'm strong enough
On my own, to stand

9-5-2015

TEARS

Listen closely to the sound
Ever closer & you'll hear
What sounds like just a falling rain
Is the noise of Heaven's tears

They seem to fall by buckets
From high up in the skies
These streams that once were teardrops
That fall from angels eyes

A sadness not forgotten
And the pain is still inflicted
The heartache & these tears
Are not, to angels eyes, restricted

They join me in my sorrow
Til clouds above me hover
Drop by drop falls down on me
No sun, my skin, to cover

Missing you so badly
To be with you is a dream
As I fear the drops become
A cold & swelling stream

For just a moment to hold you
But seconds turn to years
I'm waiting for the sun to come
And dry up all these tears

Listen closely to the sound
Of the rain and you will know
Much more with every drop that falls
I love & miss you so

3-17-2015

THE FALL

I love the color of the leaves
In autumn, all along the trees

The gentle breezes as they blow
Just not the haunting sounds as they go

I love to hear the river pass
Setting my spirit free, at last

Until the sun goes behind the hill
And the nights become cold & still

That's when it reminds me of
Someone I will always love

Someone still so dear to my heart
Who vanished & left it broken apart

Yes, I think about you every day
You know I'd have it no other way

When the colors turn to chilling blue
Here am I but where are you?

Do you ever think of me?
When you close your eyes, is it my face you see?

Even though you went away
What I feel is stronger every day

The only thought I can't erase
Is being without your precious face

The seasons change, they come & go
Til colors change & breezes blow

The time I dread more than any
The hours are short but the days feel plenty

The leaves descend, the trees go bare
Like me without you standing here

Nothing fills the space at all
You may have stumbled but I took the fall

6-17-2015
THERE IS NO DISTANCE

When I think of you
The distance fades
The sky is lit
In beautiful shades

Shades of blue
With bright, yellow sun
No rain in sight
All clouds are gone

Above the trees
My heart does soar
You're on my mind
The one I adore

The air that I breathe
My souls paradise
I see the world
When I look in your eyes

Wherever I go
There'll be no resistance
You'll be in my heart
Where there is no distance

7-4-2015
THINK OF YOU

When I think of love
I think of you
And the sweet things that
You say & do

I see the stars
That shine so bright
When I think of you
Each passing night

As over the hill
The sun makes its way
I think of you
Again today

It doesn't matter
What is the time
You are always
On my mind

No one better
Could I think of
No one else
Brings so much love

Into my heart
You fill my soul
Loving you
Is my number one goal

You deserve the best
That life has to give
I give you all
Of the life I live

You're a beautiful soul
That's shining through
When I think of love
I think of you

4-12-2015

THIS LOVE I HAVE FOR YOU

This love I have for you
My heart cannot deny
It's deeper than the oceans
And higher than the sky

It hasn't a beginning
And never will it end
Like waters of a river
It forever flows again

Its path & destination
Is always moving through
Round each & every obstacle
Until it reaches you

To love you is forever
For you deserve no less
Than every ounce of love I have
For you, my very best

My treasure that was hidden
At last, now is found
If your love was the sea
I'd be content to drown

I give to you so freely
With all I say & do
Never will my heart run dry
Of this love I have for you

6-17-2015
TO BE NEAR YOU

To be near you is a fantasy
But a dream I'll make come true
I know there is no better place
Than anywhere with you

Sometimes I feel you with me
Sometimes it's not enough
The times I am without you
The feelings get too rough

Like jagged rocks at the bottom
Of a cliff beside the sea
But I'll soar above the waters
Until your face I see

The time is swiftly passing
I swear, I almost hear you
These wings will bring me to your shore
At last, I will be near you

7-2-2015

VISION OF LOVE

A vision of love
Engulfs my mind
A vision like
No other kind

Of arms wide open
That pull me close
Keeping me company
A welcoming host

Eyes that shine
With every smile
That lead to a place
I'll stay for a while

Lips that speak
Of dreams that live
Your overflowing
Love you give

To fill my heart
And hold my spirit
If I listen closely
I even hear it

An apparition
Beautiful and true
My vision of love
My love, is you

5-16-2015

WHEEL TURNING

The wheel is turning
Time is running low
If you won't take it
Where will my love go?

The gears are grinding
It's a deafening sound
Like a bird that was soaring
And then crashed to the ground

With its wings barely moving
No flight left within
No sense of direction
No where to begin

I stand here without you
With the wind passing by
Carrying a love
That just cannot die

Bringing it to you
To lay at your feet
While the wheel is still turning
Will you take it, my sweet?

7-8-2015
YOU ARE MY LOVE

You are my love
My chosen one
The heart that beats within me
You are my rising sun

The wind that moves across me
The refreshing breeze I feel
That which my heart hungers for
A love that's true and real

The tide that rolls continuous
The waves that come in crashing
The cooling mist on a summer day
That away, my fear, is washing

The fire that warms my spirit
Within my heart it burns
That teaches me belief and trust
A lesson, each day, my mind learns

The earth on which I stand
You're all that I dream of
A fact you can depend on
You are my love

7-27-2015

YOU ONLY HAVE TO SAY YOU LOVE ME

Falling as in quicksand
Sinking in your love
Into you, my everything
What my dreams are of

Looking to the stars
Whispering your name
Dreaming of the warmth of you
Of me, do you dream the same?

Standing at the shoreline
Across an endless sea
In everything, I think of you
Do you think of me?

Are you missing me
As I am missing you?
Do you miss the things I say
And crave the things I do?

My mind gives into chaos
Thoughts race through my head
Rain falls down upon my back
Like tears the sky has shed

It understands my anguish
It knows the things I feel
Even the stars above me know
My love for you is real

I feel it in the daytime
In the coolness of the night
Even if I wanted to
This love I just can't fight

I cry out with a yearning
I reach but cannot touch
Longing to be at your side
I love you oh so much

A sleepless night surrounds me
As teardrops stain my face
Filled with all my love for you
That can never be erased

Time is swiftly passing
Before these waters rise above me
Only one thing can save me now
You only have to say you love me….

3-22-2016

2 CANDLES

2 tall candles
Were burning bright
On a cold
Dark, winter night

One was yellow
One was blue
One was me
The other was you

Waving their flames
Into the breeze
Like the leaves
Upon the trees

Burning high
And sometimes low
Giving warmth
Against the snow

Into each flame
So warm & free
Was a truth that one
Could clearly see

They were so pure
They were so bright
They were so brave
The dark to fight

Fighting on
In search of day
With their flames
To light the way

Just for a time
Were here to learn
And then their flames
Would cease to burn

Into the night
Their flames would fade
The wax would blend
Into a jade

One night, inside
The wind would pass
And penetrate
The broken glass

This night had come
The breeze blew by
One candle would live
The other would die

Less light would shine
To dark, give in
It seemed as though
The night would win

In a way
I guess it did
When 1 light was
Forever hid

Paper Flowers

1 candle left
With dimming light
On a cold
Dark, winter night

Yellow soon died
Just like the blue
I could not last
Away from you

8-12-2016

AMAYAS

You were my friend
And so much more
You were all
That I had waited for

I dreamed I held you
In my arms
All I felt
Was safe from harm

The danger of you
I didn't fear
Instead, just safe
To have you near

I held you softly
I held you close
What I felt
Was love, at most

I looked into
Your dark brown eyes
Peace and security
Was no surprise

The only thing
Of which I was afraid
Was losing the bond
That we had made

"You're beautiful!",
Was all I could say
I never knew
I could've felt that way

For a moment
That wouldn't last
Then you disappeared
Into my past

Now I cannot say
Enough about you
Just know that I
Will never doubt you

Waiting on
Your swift return
To teach me things
I want to learn

Of all the lessons
That you could teach me
Is to love again
When your arms reach me

To hold each other
In joy and peace
In prayer that
It may never cease

3-3-2016

ANGEL IN THE SNOW

One day, as children playing
We fell into the snow
Making 2 snow angels
Upon the ground below

Time went swiftly passing
The days turned into years
We met again, not randomly
You saved me from my tears

We talked & laughed together
We had our hard times, too!
I knew I'd met the twin of my soul
The moment I met you

We shared deep conversations
Not all of them were spoken
We shared a chain of friendship
That never would be broken

We bore each other's scars
Still brings a smile to me
We dreamed each other's dreams so clear
That everyone could see

You gave me a chain of your brothers
I've got it on right now
I don't know why I'm telling you this
I'm sure you know, somehow

We worked side by side
And then in different places
Telling folks about the day
We saw each other's faces

Telling them the stories
The telling never ends
Just like this never ending
Bond between 2 friends

But time with all its passing
With seasons & stormy weather
Killed our biggest, fondest dream
Of going home together

My twin, my friend & sister,
My hero & my heart
I never thought I'd see the day
That we'd be torn apart

It's hard to live with memories
Somehow, I think you know
I love & miss you more and more
My angel in the snow

8-12-2016

ASAGALEN

Soft like cotton
Against my face
Full of beauty
Full of grace

Sensual
And gratifying
Finishing
Yet undying

Intentions
With perfect speed
Patience
Like a growing seed

Vivid color
Unmistakable
Flexible
Though unbreakable

Fiery
And very wild
Then innocent
Just like a child

Bright as lightning
In the sky
Staring right
Into your eye

Determined
And unwavering
For the meat
It will be savoring

Keep alert
For it is near you
Don't fight it cause
It doesn't fear you

Now you know
You can't deny
This legend that
Will never die

6-11-2016

ASH

I didn't see it coming
I didn't hear the cry
Or recognize the footsteps
Of a wolf passing by

All I saw were bars
Of the prison I was in
Not the vivid reflection
Of a close & loyal friend

My cries must have awakened you
I didn't know you heard
I didn't know there was a sound
To the unspoken word

Then against my skin
The warmth of your caress
It took some time to notice
I simply must confess

I thought I was alone here
No solace could be found
I felt your breath upon me
And I knew you were around

To assist me in battle
Sometimes fight it for me
I admire the fire in your eyes
And, likewise, you adore me

The grayness of your coat
Your hair a soft plush
The energy I feel from you
Is a shared & subtle rush

Claws of jagged sharpness
Teeth a glowing white
Quiet in the daytime
Guarding me at night

When I feel threatened
And know I need you near
All I must do is cry wolf
And my friend, you shall appear

4-8-2016

BELIEVE IN LOVE

Drops of rain are falling
Down upon my skin
Washing away cares
Sinking deep within

Reaching into my soul
Lifting me so high
Up into the clouds
Til I could break the sky

Boundaries have vanished
No limit to this ride
Taking me through timelessness
Where I can safely hide

Stars are at my fingertips
Comets & constellations
Other souls seeking solace
And have reached their destinations

Delivered to the universe
Free to be real
Open to surroundings
Accepting what we feel

A love that is undying
Pulsating with fire
A harmony and balance
That's been my heart's desire

We search the world over
Our treasure is above
Let go of reservations
And believe in love

4-28-2016

BLOOD ON THE MOON

Til the sun burns out
And the stars shine at noon
Til the rivers run dry
And there's blood on the moon

Til the deserts are cold
And ice covers the sand
Until the prints have
Gone from my hand

This is how long
My love will last
Until the future
Meets up with the past

2-21-2016

BREAKING

Although my heart is breaking
I'll never let you go
You will always be with me
Deep inside my soul

I'll never be without you
Though, for a time, we have to part
I will be lost without you
But I will have you in my heart

We were going home together
We were happy to be going
Now the plans have altered
A bigger picture is showing

It reminds me of our meeting
Upon one summer night
An angel had come down to me
And now she must take flight

The light that burns within us
No one can possibly sever
Even though I must remain
It will not last forever

I don't know how to take this
I'm not sure what to do
You said to use my mind and heart
But my strength lies all in you

You'll never be forgotten
With all I have, I'll try
I'll do my best to make you proud
And hold my head up high

You will always be within me
In every color, hue & shade
I will keep our fire burning
And I'll never let it fade

8-28-2016

BURNING WELL

The love I feel for you inside
Is like a burning well
Watery dreams, a fiery heart
And secrets left to tell

Your smile has captured me
I rest beneath your spell
When I look into your eyes
It's like a burning well

I recall the day you said hello
I remember it so clear
The words you said to me just seemed
To vanish all my fear

Then you said, "My dear, I love you."
It rang just like a bell
Now the love I feel for you inside
Is like a burning well

Will you always love me, dear?
Can you tell me true?
Do you think about me
The way I think of you?

Will your love fade out for me
Like a star that's fell?
Or does it blaze inside your heart
Like a burning well?

6-11-2016
CASTING STONES

A beginning but no end
This stone that I carry
Drawing down my energy
The carrying leaves me weary

For scores I've pulled it
Behind me & all around
Sometimes I stumble
And am down on the ground

You cannot see it
You say it isn't there
It's a product of my past, you say
And you refuse to hear

How real the struggle is
How tight the rope is pulled
You're blinded by your own stones
And by them you are fooled

Before you send judgement
And blame this on my past
See the rocks you drag behind
How many stones can you cast?

6-11-2016

CHAINS

I dream of the day
I pass through the portal
When I break this shell
And become immortal

To cast off this cage
That surrounds and confines me
It's what is within it
That truly defines me

What is without
Is nothing I cling to
There's another song
My spirit sings to

Music only
The soul can hear
It lifts me up
And draws me near

To the place
My soul knows well
Where heavenly beings
And Angels dwell

Where a river flows
And darkness can't be
No shadows
Only light I'll see

Time has left me
Weak and broken
Filled up inside
With prayers unspoken

In hopes that soon
They will be heard
Even though I haven't
Said a word

I pray that love
Will not forsake me
And free me from what
Tries to break me

Break me but
Will not set me free
This thing some say
Was brought on me

Rescue me from
This thing that drains
Hear my call
And break these chains

3-21-2016

CIRCLE AND A CHAIN

A chain's around my neck
It's fastened to a ring
A silver fascination
Hanging on a string

Some have asked me what it is
Others simply stare
I soothe their curiosity
When I tell them why it's there

My best friend gave it to me
It was someone's very dear
It was her baby brothers
He is no longer here

She wanted me to have it
She thought he'd want that too
I wear it with pride & honor
The way that he would do

The moment that I put it on
The blind could even see
We arose above a friendship
And became a family

I tell folks she's my sister
Because in my heart she is
Our brother is even happy
When I wear this chain of his

It represents the 2 of us
A ring without an end
And after we have passed away
It will all begin again

A chain that can't be broken
This is who we are
If proof is what you're looking for
You don't have to look that far

The ring binds us together
Like the heart of God, so strong
A love that is eternal
Like music to a song

Like water is to flowers
Or leaves upon a tree
Like the shore is to the ocean
So is she to me

When I'm feeling lost
Like I just can't fight the pain
My strength is made apparent
By a circle and a chain

5-5-2016

COLORBLIND

The wonders of a rainbow
The colors of the sky
The prism of the rain
As the wind passes by

The tallness of the trees
Leaves an emerald green
The deep blue ocean waters
These things are so serene

When you look around you
Think of what you see
Picture what is staring back
Think of what could be

Waiting in the distance
In the shadows standing still
Wonder what's illusion
Determine what is real

Turn your eyes toward me
Am I in your sight?
Do you know the difference
Between the day & night?

Can you hear the thunder?
Can you see the rain?
Can you feel what I feel or
Are all your senses strained?

Maybe you're not looking
Or maybe it's just me
Maybe you're just colorblind
And I'm not what you see

3-3-2016

EVERY SHADE OF BLUE

When the clouds gather round me
And rain refuses to fall
The only voice I'll hear will be mine
When your dear name I call

I feel the sun is setting
I fear when it will rise
What if it brings the day
I no longer see your eyes?

Or look you in the face
Or hear you speak to me
When I go to sleep at night
Will it be you I see?

You're all I've ever known
Nothing was before you
The instant we made eye contact
I knew that I adored you

You're everything I came to be
All I'll ever know
Soon I'll be lost without you
When it's your time to go

No stars will fill my sky
There'll be no gentle breezes
With such a devastating loss
The mind never eases

What am I to do
What will life be then
How long will it take me
To learn to live again

What am I without you
Only half, it's true
After this I'll only be
Every shade of blue

6-28-2016

FACE THE RAIN

Alone is where I find myself
Surrounded by your grace
To share the good times & the bad
Or just to seek your face

To ask so many questions
No answers can I find
For you to open up my eyes
That sometimes seem so blind

To comfort me in dark places
To celebrate the good
Just to be my shield & guard
Even though you said you would

Many times I feel unworthy
Sometimes I'm just not able
To fight this daily battle
Still, you welcome me to your table

Without you, I am nothing
What hope have I to be?
Without my hand in yours
I'll never become free

This my cry, oh lord, to you
The reason I came here
I've found myself alone again
In an ocean of my tears

I know that I am nothing
At least, I'm not without you
I know your promises are true
My heart could never doubt you

I just feel better asking
I know that you'll be there
When my time comes to cross over
I know I am prepared

When the dark of night surrounds me
And seeks to cause me pain
When the sun has hidden its face from me
Together we'll face the rain

4-21-2016

FREE (2016)

The captains ship is spotless all around
No finer vessel on the sea can be found

It picked me up some time ago, you see
When I was in danger, it set me free

I was stranded on an island, all alone
Far from happiness few others have known

I looked around but could not see too clear
My comfort was close to me. So, so near

I saw a light in the distance shining
As my soul in darkness was repining

My eyes looked up to see the flag flying
At last, the dread of death, too, was dying

A lifeline was thrown. It took hold of me
Now I sail the captains ship. I am free

4-1-2016

FULFILLING YOUR WISH

Just like all other times
You are on my mind
As I stare at the clock
Fearing when it will unwind

Pictures of our time
Race throughout my brain
While I race the hands of time
With no regret or refrain

Though some things I haven't done
And words I've left unsaid
The wind is getting colder
My sweat turns into dread

Sands of time are falling
The hourglass is filling
While my mind burns in agony
I feel my skin chilling

Spring turns into summer
The summer drifts to fall
The cold of winter scares me
And I beg for it to stall

Hoping you will warm me
Praying you can see
That being here without you
Is no place for me

On the edge of falling
From this cliff of grief
Looking out across forever
And the past in disbelief

The breezes cease to play
The flowers will not dance
Songs of time are silent
Yet in my head they prance

Taunting me severely
Breaking me into
It's difficult to fathom
A life lived without you

Fearing the clocks unwinding
I feel your time is near
I choke on thoughts of solitude
And time without you here

Cloaked in cloths of sadness
In chains from dusk till dawn
I will walk a path of daydreams
Fulfilling your wish to go on

3-29-2016

GINNY

I haven't forgotten
The laughs that we shared
I haven't looked over
The way that you cared...

...For so many people
Your work & the town
How you spread your
Happiness all around

Or being in your home
On a sunny afternoon
And parting with a heartfelt
"I'll see you soon."

Then on a Sunday,
A cold, lonesome day
You, so suddenly
Were taken away

I was to be there
If I could redo
That day
There would've been 2

Or maybe if I had
You'd still be here
Maybe I'd hear
Your voice real clear

Teaching me things
Like you used to do
With a warm smile
That was uniquely you

Wishful thoughts
How I wish some were more
But fate
Had different things in store

More than 23 years
And in my heart you live
Though your life
You had to give

I'm thankful for you
Though my tears are many
After all this time
I still miss you, Ginny

In memory of Ginny Gilpatrick

4-24-2016

GLANCING THROUGH CLOUDS

His call rang out early
He was rising like the sun
Going ever higher since
The day he had begun

Songs of love & light
Of peace & war alike
Riding through the winds
On his purple bike

Touching many lives
All throughout his career
Mine was one of those
The memories are clear

Listening to old songs
And new ones with delight
Memorizing titles
Inspiring me to write

Even in his absence
He still draws the crowds
Now he rests above the rain
Glancing through the clouds

Inspired by & in memory of
Prince (1958 - 2016)

8-9-2016

GOODBYE (2016)

I hear the clocks loud ticking
Its thunderous step & rhyme
A bittersweet melody
I'm running out of time

Like sands in the glass are falling
Each grain a memory
Years of sand has fallen
The glass is you & me

With no hope of it breaking
To free us from this curse
To give the sun its playground
And let the clouds disperse

The cold moon now is rising
The morning brings the dew
Golden teardrops on the ground
At the thought of losing you

I hear the clocks loud ticking
The Lightning breaks the sky
Reflecting off my tears
As I have to say goodbye

4-6-2016

HEARTS ACROSS THE OCEAN

For years I dreamed about you
Without a name or face
I dreamed about a people
From some other place

I dreamed about a river
And of the mountains high
Yet I dreamed about a place
Where hearts would never die

I didn't understand it
I couldn't see beyond the cliffs
How God was getting ready
To bless me with a gift

Although I heard a language
I could not understand
I could hear it with my heart
That there was a special plan

And I'm forever grateful
The timing was just right
That I received your message
On a breezy April night

Hearts across the ocean
Hands beyond the sea
Reaching through the distance
Joining you & me

2-29-2016
HEARTS PRAYER

Now I lay me down to sleep
But I think of you & start to weep
My thoughts run wild and fast and free
Full of the fear of you leaving me
If I should die before I wake
I ask my God my soul to take
That I may again spend time with you
Like times before as we used to do
If I should live for other days
I'll face the sun and its warming rays
And thank my God in word & mind
For you & our very short time

6-25-2016

HIDDEN

Even the sun hides its face from me.

And on those rare days
When it does touch my skin,
It runs like water off my arms

The rays slide down from the
Blue sky but they fall to the
Ground, as if a shield has been
Placed around my body

Dark glasses do shield my eyes
From the light but nothing shields
My heart

What else looks away as I pass by?

When the sun trades places with the
Moon and stars, will they run away?

Will rivers flow around me?

Will the seeds in the earth refuse
To grow when I walk on the
Ground they sleep beneath?

These things, too, will pass away

I will remain & these things that have
Run from me, I shall embrace!

Some day, even my words will shine.
They will glow like beams from the moon,
Sparkle like the stars & all that now is lost from me,
Again,
Will not be....
Hidden!

1-28-2016

HOLD ON

Hold on with all you have
Don't ever let me go
Deep inside yourself, somehow
I think you truly know

You're half of who I am
The second part of me
When I feel I've lost my way
It's you who helps me see

You guide my every footstep
I hold and never fall
I never lose my balance
I cling to you, my all

I look across the waters
The only thing I find
Is a love that is undying
And is so far from blind

You see me for who I am
Mistakes are all included
You accept my every failure
And not to what I've eluded

I see you within my eyes
I see myself in you
I never have to question
I know just what to do

Paper Flowers | 213

Bless the day the sun arose
And brought me to the dawn
God gave me you to love
My hope, I will hold on

5-4-2016

HOLDING TO MY MEMORIES

Been sorting out my memories
There's one that clouds my mind
When you went missing long ago
And left my love behind

Over a year later
I had you in my sight
But you had to walk away again
And leave me there that night

An ocean filled with dreams
I was left to sort through
Walking streets of memories
Of times I spent without you

Looking up at streetlights
As the rain falls in my eyes
I wrap my coat around me
But my heart has no disguise

It's open like a window
On a warm, spring day
Waiting on the breezes
Of your love to come my way

Holding to my memories
It's hard to hold this pain
I'm missing you so deeply
Like the deserts miss the rain

6-26-2016

HOW IT FEELS

Falling in love
I know how it feels
I know how it hurts
I know how it heals

I know the things
It puts you through
I know the tragedies
And triumphs too

When to hold on
When to let go
All these things
I truly know

How it destroys
How it creates
How it dreads
And anticipates

I've felt its truths
I've heard its lies
Been blinded by
Its thin disguise

I watched it weave
Its cruel spell
It raised me high
And then I fell

Deep in love
My heart it steals
All these things
Are how it feels

I know these things
That they are true
I've found myself
In love with you

3-1-2016

IN EVERYTHING, YOUR HEART

In everything
I do and see
His loving voice
Is guiding me

To a place
I've never known
Where the chill of wind
Has never blown

Where the sun arose
But has not set
Where all is peace
And no regret

Where ocean waters
Meet the shore
Where I'll always find
An open door

Where I know
There'll always be
A place for you
A place for me

With a shallow sea
Of bright green fields
Where there shall be
No swords or shields

There'll be no war
But only love
In this place
So high above

The only sword
Will be a word
That cuts with kindness
We've never heard

No tears, no pain
No grief nor death
Just life maintained
By God's own breath

One day, this place
Our eyes shall see
Our hearts and minds
Will then be free

There we'll make
A brand new start
Receive it
Open up your heart

3-22-2016

INSIDE YOUR EYES

I see myself
Inside your eyes
Nothing to hide
With no disguise

Who I am
I'm free to be
The same goes when
You look at me

You see you
For who you are
No casting hope
Upon a star

I love you
For who's inside
I couldn't stop
Not if I tried

The sun shines bright
The flowers bloom
Love lives when
You're in the room

Then just when I
Least expect it
My love shines
And you reflect it

Shining out from
Deep inside you
Like a treasure
I want to hide you

I find myself
When my heart cries
Surrounded by love
Inside your eyes

8-13-2016

ISLAND IN THE SKY

I was on an island
And you were far from me
The next time I would see you
Felt like eternity

You were thinking of me
I could hear you in my sleep
Summoning me home
Across the ocean deep

4 days on the water
Making my way through
Hearing songs that reminded me
How much I was missing you

"I Will Wait For You" was one
"I'm Free" was another
As I clung to a chain
That used to be your brothers

It felt like a month
But only a week had passed
That I waited just to tell you
That I was home at last

I finally got to talk to you
I wasn't well prepared
To hear the news you gave me
I felt alone & scared

You were running out of time
Breaking your shield & dome
Preparing to spread your wings
And make your way back home

I surely knew I'd miss you
How could all this be?
While you thought that I had left you,
You were leaving me

We wouldn't go together
As we thought so long ago
But we are one now & forever
It's just hard to let you go

Soon you're taking your trip
I'll watch you sailing by
Having YOUR vacation
On an island in the sky

6-28-2016

LIGHT IN DARK PLACES

I wanna be your
Light in a dark place
I want to bask in your warmth
And see your face

I want our hands to join
Our hearts to beat as one
I want to walk beside you
Until our days are done

I want to be the music
For the song that you sing
I want to be
Your everything

I want to spend your days with you
I want you in mine
I want to be the light, my gem
That causes you to shine

I want to be your armor
That shields you in your fight
I want to be your day
I want to be your night

I want to be your equal
Though that could never be
There are no others like you
At least there's not to me

Just as a Deck of cards
We could be the aces
We could be each other's
Light in dark places

8-11-2016

LOVE THAT SMILE

I love that smile
I love those eyes
They have the power
To hypnotize

To make me melt
Like late winter snow
To take me where
I long to go

Into your world
By word or deed
To be by you
Is all I need

To raise me up
To a place that's higher
To forever stay
Is my desire

In a field of flowers
To lay by you
So tell me what
You'd have me do

To remain with you
Under star lit skies
To lose myself
In your sparkling eyes

So one more time
Just for a while
Warm me by
Your loving smile

2-9-2016
LOVING YOU

Night is personal
Day is not
Left to live
With what each brought

Left to swim
In silent seas
Left to fall
On bended knees

Floating on a raft
Of fate
To drink the drink
We say we hate

To swallow all
Our foolish pride
And accept the fact
That hope has died

Died & left us
All alone
By ourselves
For it's all gone

The needle pushes
Hope flows in
False beliefs
Now let's pretend

That everything
Is fine again
All these years
Down the drain?

No, I've learned
I've walked the walk
Listened close
And TAUGHT the talk

The time is now
The time is here
Know I'll
Always miss you dear

My promise
I will carry on
Loving you
Is all I've known

3-13-2016

MISSING YOU

Missing you so badly now
My words just can't convey
How I long to tell you
How I wish for one more day

I see your name I've written
I hear you in my mind
Still, nothing would make me happier
Than to see you one more time

I know that cannot happen
That wish cannot come true
I'm just a wandering soul down here
Since the day that I lost you

Since the day that you were taken
Even though you wished to go
I've walked this path alone
And miss you more than you could know

You are the other half of me
I can't exist without you
Even though you said I could
And I said I'd never doubt you

This space you left within me
No one could ever fill
I love you like no other
I miss you & always will

3-3-2016

MY EAGLE

My eagle soon is soaring
Beyond the land and sea
High above the heavens
And far away from me

Leaving me alone here
As she sails into the air
There are no other eagles
With such shine & flare

No others were before her
No others will there be
No form will fill the empty space
She's leaving deep in me

I will go upon my journey
But when I look into the sky
I'll no longer see my eagle
Flying safely by

The sky will then be vacant
The blue will turn to gray
The sun will hide its face from me
Until I fade away

But even the willow bends
It bends yet rarely breaks
Such will be the heart in me
No matter how it aches

One day will see its breaking
And leave my spirit regal
When it breaks beyond this shell
And I rise to meet my eagle

4-1-2016

MY SWEET ROSE

In these eyes
Filled with a vision
Of my love for you
My hearts best decision

A choice influenced
By the skies above
That seem endless
Such for you, is my love

Even when the clouds
Above me hover
They cannot overshadow
More love to discover

Your eyes, like stars
Into my soul, shine
Reminding my heart
That you're forever mine

I'm yours, as well
Like the suns shining rays
I will remain faithful
And fill your longest days

Just as you fill mine
So long ago I chose
To shine my love
Upon you, my sweet rose

2-28-16

ON OUR WAY

We've waited for a lifetime
Looking for the day
When our lights would shine as one
And we'd be on our way

That time is soon arriving
Our fears have all been faced
Everything that's hurt us
From our minds, will be erased

We've waded many rivers
Crossed every field and plain
To places we have never known
And, to others, can't explain

We've borne each other's scars
Shared each pain, dream & thought
Had simultaneous happenings
And lived the bond they've brought

Still we take it with us
No matter where we go
No secrets stand between us
What I know, you also know

You know everything about me
And I also know you
We are 1 now & forever
Our bond is strong and true

That day is soon upon us
Without one, the other can't stay
Let us join our hearts and spirits
Come, let's be on our way

2-20-2016

ONE SOUL

You will always be with me,
My friend & so much more
When I felt all hope was gone
You opened up the door

You'll always be my heart,
My soul & my best friend
I'll never be alone again
Our bond will never end

I know you will come back for me
I looked for you so long
When I was at my weakest
Your love then made me strong

Wherever you go off to
I know you won't be far
I'll look into the heavens
And there, I'll see your star

When the day comes and I leave here
Not sure when that will be
A light will pierce the darkness
Your face, again, I'll see

I will wait to hear you calling
When your wings around me fold
To carry me back home with you
Then we shall be one soul

8-9-2016
ONE STAR

A new star shines
It bears your name
The feeling it brings
Seems quite the same

As the love I feel
That shines for you
In everything
I say and do

I noticed it
In the cool night air
While engaged
In a midnight prayer

For something sweet
To fill the space
But nothing else
Can take your place

Two bodies
One soul
Yet somehow
My heart you stole

We walk together
On a single path
I'd freely give
Everything I have

Again to walk
These steps we take
As I speak
I feel my heart break

Soon you'll fly
It won't be the same
As I see the star
That bears your name

To rise and fly
Into the air
Will be my hearts
Most sincere prayer

That we will live
In the sky, so far
As a single soul
Upon one star

3-21-2016
ONLY FOR YOU

Only for you
This game do I play
To win your love
Over each day

To reach out to you
And get you to see
That you're
The only one for me

The only one
I could ever choose
That I could never
Stand to lose

I think of you
Each day & night
It fills my mind
With pure delight

When thoughts of you
Come passing by
All that I can do
Is try

With all I am
And all I can be
I try to send you
Thoughts of me

I'll win your love
You know it's true
And my love, my love
Is only for you

3-24-2016

OVER THE WALL

This castle that they see
Is just a house of cards
There are no jewels
There are no guards

There is a tower
Where a raven calls
Perched above
These fragile walls

Looking down
Upon the frame
Taunting me
As it screams my name

I hold my head
To block the sound
Though it echoes til
It touches the ground

Outside eyes
Cannot see through
They're unaware
Of all I view

How do I tell them
What do I say?
They've never seen me
Quite this way

They've no idea
That I'm not strong
They believe I am
But they are wrong

I want to explain
But I throw a curve
I feel that's not
What they deserve

This house of cards
Is destined to fall
The truth will spill out
Over the wall

3-3-2016

PATRICIA (2016)

You are my inspiration
My thoughts of you are dear
I don't know where I'd be
If I didn't have you here

You rescued me from danger
I was so lost & down
You gave me hope to cling to
That day you came around

I won't forget our meeting
I cherish it each day
We'd known each other times before
It could've been no other way

We sat down at the table
Then saw each other's eyes
We knew each other instantly
It wasn't a surprise

A light shown from within us
And glowed before our faces
Taking us to times gone by
And to familiar places

I felt I was your equal
As though we'd met again
Like we were a single soul
Living life as twins

Others stood around us
Amazed by what they saw
Things we'd do and say alike
Without a single flaw

Each of us were asked
When apart, about the other
I always said, "my sister"
You always said, "my brother"

If you got cut, I bled
Sometimes, I'd have your scar
We'd look into the sky
And wish on the same star

What more could I wish for
What else could there be
I got more than I deserved
When God gave you to me

7-1-2016

PETALS ON THE GROUND

A rose in bloom
But for how long?
Days are short
Timing is wrong

I hold on tight
It seems I slip
I've sailed so long
On this lonesome ship

The oceans wide
The sea is deep
I cannot close
My eyes and sleep

The waters rage
The storm moves on
The sun sets slow
I see no dawn

May the sun
For me, wait to rise
And dry the tears
That fall from my eyes

May I hear
Your call and sound
And not leave
Petals on the ground

That this rose
For you may grow
And greater joy
I'll come to know

5-2-2016

PICTURE OF YOU

Long ago
When it was new
I fell in love
With a picture of you

I took it out
And cut around it
Happy enough
That I had found it

I've thought of you
For many long years
Through hardships and triumphs
Through laughter and tears

I wondered where
You could've gone
And each time I thought of you,
Could you have known?

Known that you
Were on my mind
Could you see me
Or was your love blind?

Blind to dreams
I held in my heart
Beginning the day
That we had to part

The day you left
And went so far
My wish broke into
With a falling star

A star that crashed
When it fell on the ground
I frantically searched
But you couldn't be found

Found that I may
Tell you I love you
And that no other soul
Could I see above you

I looked & I searched
But just couldn't see
If there was someone else
Or were you for me

Maybe you weren't
Could it be, was it true
Could I handle
My life without you?

More time passed
I searched earth & sky
While watching the days
And the years going by

And then just today
When hope seemed to be through
At last, I'd found
A new picture of you

Beautiful
As you were years ago
And all those old dreams
Were starting to grow

If these words I've written
Someday you should read
Know all these years
That I've loved you, indeed

If more years should pass
And hope has us in store
Know that I'll only
Love you much more

Until that time comes
Before today is through
I'll be falling in love
With a new picture of you

2-5-2016
RED, RED ROSES

You were my vessel
Sailing wild and free
You were my guiding star
Shining down on me

You were my treasure
My chest of gold
You were riches from
Stories untold

You were the spring
You were the fall
In my eyes
You were it all

The summertime
The winters chill
The candles warmth
That I could feel

Everything you were
To me
The calming brook
The raging sea

The mountain that never
Stood in my way
The valley I walked
Gladly, each day

The level ground
On which I stood
The thoughts I thought
And knew I should

My gift from God
My all in all
Whenever you stumbled
I took the fall

Everything you are
And so much more
Now I'm waiting
Our bond to restore

Our shared dream
Our common goal
Our joined hearts
And single soul

When I go to sleep
Each night
Though my eyes are closed
You'll be in my sight

I'll never forget you
My mind never doses
Thinking of you
And your red, red roses

5-26-2016

ROSES IN THE RAIN

Just like the roses
First meet the rain
I know that I
Will see you again

I miss you more
Than you will know
But like the rose
You continue to grow

Each day that comes
Though rain or shine
I miss the days
When you were mine

Missing all
The times we shared
How I felt
Just knowing you cared

Your love so strong
Embraces all of us
Always felt
Whether or not discussed

Your sweetness unmatched
Your smile so your own
The love that you left
Still is shown

A legacy you left
A life of love
An angel sent
From heaven above

You will be loved
You will be missed
Like a rose
The rain has kissed

A rose in heaven
In God's bouquet
With a beauty
Only you display

Forever we'll love you
For love has no end
Til the roses meet
The rain again

4-7-2016
RUNAWAY HEART

At the edge of the sky
The sun is sinking
The silent colors
Leave me thinking...

...Of you, my love
And days gone by
As another day drips
Beneath the sky

Like an ocean of tears
That have rained down
Soaking deep
Into the ground

Seeds of sadness
Springing forth
Blooming love
For what it's worth

Sweetness falls,
Rains down my face
You fill my heart
I feel it race

To a beat
The flowers dance to
I'd love you again
If I had the chance to

I'd do it all
Over & over,
My lucky charm,
My 4 leafed clover

My shining one,
My hearts prize
Glowing like
A star in my eyes

Thoughts of you
Everywhere abound
I get high on you
And can't come down

I don't want to
I want to stay
In your arms
Just 1 more day

For you, my love
That's just a start
For you, I have
A runaway heart

3-24-2016

SCHIZOAFFECTIVE

I didn't want you
To see me like this
I wanted you to believe
Everything was bliss

But I cannot keep
This thing at bay
It haunts me day
By endless day

These thoughts & visions
And voices I hear
Make me wish
That you were near

To drive away
This force, unkind
That to which
I'm sometimes blind

I don't know
Where it comes from
It's sometimes quiet
Then loud as a drum

Shadows pass
The room, they fill
Moving about
And are never still

Frightening thoughts
I cannot fight
That come to me
Both day and night

Feels like a cage
Is holding me
I want to break out
I want to be free

They say, I've heard
That time heals all
But not even time
Will silence this call

I run & I run
Yet still it is there
Following me
Everywhere

I count the days
And time it will take
For this horrifying
Glass to break

8-14-2016

SEARCH FOR LIGHT

I need your light tonight
For mine is growing dim
You are my only hope
My rescue, my gem

I've found myself in darkness
Just a spark out in the distance
I reach out in desperation
I only receive resistance

I'm too far away
Without even a beam
I beg for safety
I pray this is a dream

I know that this is certain
And not at all strange
I know that things can turn around
I know that this can change

Just when I think the end is near
And I find my lifeboat sinking
I reach out for your hand
Now from the cup of life I'm drinking

Your light now shines upon me
And with your light the darkness dies
At last, things are not hopeless
You will dry these tears from my eyes

You were all that I needed
When the skies were black as coal
Now my fears have vanished
And your light burns in my soul

3-21-2016

SOMETIMES IT'S JUST YOUR VOICE

Sometimes I think about you
Sometimes it's hard to try
Sometimes it's just your voice
That makes me want to cry

An overwhelming feeling
Like I've never felt before
As wings breaking through the sky
I pray to feel it more

I want to stand before you
Like the foam upon the sea
And fall upon your shore
Right where I long to be

I want to walk the pathway
I'm so afraid I'll fall
Still, I will stand ready
And waiting for your call

Because sometimes I crave you
My spirit has no choice
Sometimes it's just your love for me
Sometimes it's just your voice

3-1-2016

STORM

A storm inside me rages
While outside I see the rain
Bleeding down from heaven
Leaving a crimson stain

A stain within my being
A mark upon my mind
My world around me crashes in
And seems to be unkind

But a peace is left within me
That world can't take away
Even when the storm is strong
There's coming a brighter day

Right now the clouds are hovering
The wind picks up its speed
But a rose will grow when the storm has passed
It cannot drown the seed

A thunder roars inside me
So long now I have fought
I'm reminded just how strong He is
And to fight with all I've got

No matter how bright the Lightning
To fear I will not conform
For, at last, this rain shall pass
God's stronger than my storm

4-19-2016

STRINGS

I used to be a puppet
Bound by many strings
Doing what I was told
And kept from many things

I wished to be real
Free from strings & such
I thought I wanted freedom
And wanted it so much

One day that wish was granted
My time had been served
I thought I was getting
What I so deserved

That day I had met you
My strings were gone
I could be a freer me
My life could go on

We shared sweet times together
Freely, I did live
A heart full of love for you
I freely had to give

Then one day you left me
Another you had found
All my loving feelings
Were scattered on the ground

I'd built my life around you
But now you'd gone away
No love left to give
I prayed for that old day

When my heart was a patch
On this puppets wooden frame
And I would hurt no longer
Or remember your name

I went to sleep one night
On a bed of regret
Oh how I was wishing
Your face I could forget

I woke up in the morning
With an empty heart of wood
No knowledge of my heartache
Like I wished I could

Once I was a puppet
No heart, emotions or things
Just laying in someone's arms
Bound by their hearts strings

3-13-2016

TEAR TRACKS

Angel in the hallway
Angel by my door
Walked in through my sorrow
And left tear tracks on the floor

She knew that I was hurting
I swear, she felt the pain
She was summoned by my spirit
As I thought about her name

She walked around the corner
And asked me what I wanted
I could not find an answer
I felt the place was haunted

Invaded by a whisper
A gentle voice I heard
She spoke in a choir of voices
Yet she never said a word

She only saw me standing
At the sidelines in my sadness
Suddenly, all of that dispersed
And faded in to gladness

With just the look in her eyes
And a smile upon her face
The room lit in her majesty
And filled the empty space

She reached her hand out to me
And handed me a smile
Everything just disappeared
And left me for a while

We shared sweet times together
Though only for a season
Then she had to go away
I guess God had a reason

He took my angel from me
Far as the eye could see
But everything I needed
She had left inside of me

Hope that I could cling to
A promise from above
Even though I miss her
I'm surrounded by her love

A light down through the hallway
A shadow on my door
A comfort deep within me and
No tear tracks on the floor

5-3-2016

THAT NIGHT

White walls in my memory
Full of flowers blue
Nearby sounds of trains
All lead me back to you

On a hot summer night
I dreamed of something more
I awoke to see your shadow
Come passing through my door

A new dream I was dreaming
A vision from the sky
I didn't question its reason
I did not ask it why

I opened up my heart
To receive it coming in
I peered into the darkness
And there I found a friend

I found a new creation
That I had never seen
I found new strength awakening
Outside this endless dream

I remember things I felt that night
I see it all so clear
Like a new beginning
I stepped out of my fear

I stepped out of the darkness
And passed into the light
Lifting ever higher
Into a star-filled night

I walked the path of angels
Lit with lights in blue
I experienced heaven on earth
The night I spent with you

Flying through billowing clouds
Cold & fire sensations
Passing through many places
Without a destination

Dreading coming down
From this journey we were on
Reaching for the midnight
Descending into dawn

I awoke to white walls
Blue flowers all around
Clouds beneath my feet
When I stepped on to the ground

This is what it felt like,
My dream in day lit sky
This is what I think of
When I think of you and I

8-10-2016

THE BEAUTIFUL ONE

A rose from heaven's garden
A ray as from the sun
Like music out of silence
My beautiful one has come

A golden light surrounds you
So bold it tames the winds
Softer than a gentle breeze
And a peace to me it sends

A smile that's like no other
A love deep as the sea
Fashioned by the hands of God
To my heart, you are the key

That unlocks a dream within me
Opening up a door
For as long as I recall
You're all that I've wished for

My light forever shining
My rose kissed by the dew
Everywhere that I could go
Leads me back to you

I long to tell your story
Though sometimes my words may fail
Compared to you, my shining one
All of the others pale

I look into your eyes
To where your love comes from
And know deep down inside my soul
That my beautiful one has come

1-13-2016

THE NEXT BIG THING

I roamed side streets of Jamaica
I lounged on a private isle
I got to leave all life behind
And be free for a while

I walked barefoot on the sand
I found a tiny shell
I've found there's so much more to life
Stories left to tell

Brotherhood forgotten
Blinded by color of skin
Hope that lives within all hearts
To be discovered again

I went to see the ocean
I felt the mist of the sea
Yet something so much more than this
Captivated me

The smiles on strangers faces
The joy within their eyes
Opened enough to be themselves
While closed to little lies

Children not impressed
By design & sleekness
Radiating pure delight
From their own uniqueness

Everything broken down
Nothing complicated
Living life to impress
Is way too overrated

It's who we are within
That makes the world alive
To lift each other up in life
Should be that for which we strive

When you hear the music
You've got a song to sing
Live life for the moment
And not the next big thing

2-29-2016

THE RAIN

Even the angels
Dread the day
When from my life
You go away

Every time
I feel that fear
Another angel
Sheds a tear

Falling down
One at a time
On this aching
Heart of mine

To the skies
I cast my gaze
One by one
I'm losing days

Days that I
Can be with you
But there's nothing that
My heart can do

I feel that fear
That you are going
With no warning
No way of knowing

Another tear
An angel's shed
As thoughts of you
Race through my head

The storm moves in
The angels weep
Knowing you,
I cannot keep

You will go
As I'll remain
And as I walk away
I'll feel the rain

3-3-2016

THE STONE

I know the time is coming
I know that it is close
I know I'll feel your final breath
That's not what hurts me most

The flood of years of memories
The flashing points in time
Seeing all our days go by
Is not what grips my mind

Looking at your pictures
Not being able to call
All that wishful thinking
No, that's not it at all

Those things may hurt me deeply
More with every passing day
Plus the things I wanted to say to you
That I never got to say

Reading my own words back
No matter what my fears
Will now & forever leave me
Fighting back the tears

Hearing songs we both loved
The movie that was us
Knowing that I need to talk
But nothing's to discuss

Not one of these occasions,
Not a single one
Will be the moment that I feel
Broken and undone

But the one thing that will pierce me
When I'm standing there alone
Will be the last words that you left with me
Carved upon your stone

3-3-2016

VOID

This place that you are leaving
Will never be the same
Already, there's a loneliness
From calling out your name

You so greatly will be missed
That sweet smile on your face
The memories that we've made
From my heart, won't be erased

They'll stay with me forever
While on this earth I roam
I'll bring them safely with me
When my time comes to go home

Watch over me each moment
Lest my heart should be destroyed
By the emptiness inside it
The lonesome, hollow void

3-30-2016

WHEN LONELINESS DIES

The oceans are still
The waves do not roll
Upon my heart
Death takes its toll

Like a ship on the sea
You drift away
As I stand on the shore
Only to pray

As I watch you
Sail from my view
Knowing only
My heart is for you

Your hand within mine
Loosens its hold
The only price to pay
Is tears of gold

Gold like memories
I hold of you close
Of all my treasures
I shall miss you most

The loss of you
Will carry the reflection
Of my love for you
And my hearts affection

The day comes soon
I will be with you
Then I, too
Will sail from view

Your hand, again
I will hold in mine
At the edge of the sea
Where the sun does shine

I shall drift away
On a ship of my own
With flashes of you
And our love that has grown

For you, I am only
Though my heart now cries
I shall then join you
When loneliness dies...

2-29-2016

WHERE FLOWERS DON'T DIE

Each day I wish
Upon a star
Without a doubt
Of where you are

For deep within
My heart, so strong
Is where you are
And do belong

I walk a path
That's sometimes rough
But I know your love
Is more than enough

To get me by
And see me through
As only you
Could ever do

I hear your voice
I see your cross
I feel at peace
And not at loss

With all my soul
And heart, I'll try
To be with you
Where flowers don't die

6-11-2016

WRITER

To entertain
Or teach a lesson
To leave you guessing
Or let you question

My harmless inspiration
Or point intended
Coax your curiosity
Not leave you offended

Like an actor
On a stage
It's my job
To shake the cage

To lure memories
Or provoke a thought
Joy, love, happiness
Whatever my words brought

Sometimes made up
Though sometimes real
Depending upon
What you feel

I paint with words
A colorful mixture
The finished product
An original picture

I'm a writer
I don't regret it
Even if you're unsure
Or completely get it

6-26-2016

YELLOW LIGHT

Like a candle
Without a flame
Like someone who
Doesn't know their name

I'd be lost without you
If you had to go
I'd forget all that
I used to know

Nothing would matter
At least not to me
But I know
You wish to be free

You've dreamed of going
For many years
I've noticed your pain
And felt your tears

You race the clock
Look for the day
You pray & wish
Your time away

Your life is short
Don't rush it by
Don't move so fast
Do not ask why

Stop & take
The time to see
You are
Everything to me

You run too fast
Just take it slow
Until your green light
Lets you go

Until that time
Just hold on tight
Give caution to
The yellow light

3-22-2016

YOU'LL NEVER KNOW

If I could only tell you
If I could only show
Just how much I love you
But, my love, you'll never know

I could talk forever
And still could never say
How my heart longs for you
And I love you more each day

No amount of talking
There's nothing I could give
To provide a worthy token
Of this love I can't outlive

I'll try my best to tell you
I'll work to make it show
But just how much I love you
I'm afraid you'll never know

2-24-2017

7 NEW WORLDS

They say there are 7 new worlds
That science has discovered
Plenty of wonderful things out there
Soon to be uncovered

The rich will toast each other
The stars shine brighter there
Or so I'm told in these worlds of gold
So high up in the air

Cruises will be boat rides
Planes mere crop dusters
Diamonds will be silly next
To those celestial clusters

Where caviar is junk food
Wine a tasteless liquid
Things held sacred here are
In danger of being wicked

The skies are expanding
Delights are ever increasing
Delicacies here on earth
Will barely be pleasing

Everyone with their eyes on the sky
Awaiting the next big thing
Nothing is enough anymore
This world has lost its bling

While everyone runs crazy
We all can see it's true
I could never be distracted from
My world that's here with you

3-6-2017

AT ALL

When you say you love me
Is it just a simple thing
Or do you say it like a doll
When someone pulls a string

Do you really feel it
Is it even there to show
Can you find it in your heart
To simply let me know

Do I have to make a guess
Is there any love for me
If it's even in your heart
Why won't you let me see

Don't toy with my emotions
Cause I'm not that lifeless doll
Let me know or let me go
If you've any love at all

Inspired by Paper Doll by Fleetwood Mac

3-6-2017

BECAUSE OF YOU

I looked for you not knowing
I looked but couldn't see
That somewhere in the distance
You also looked for me

We each were broken pieces
2 halves that made a soul
Neither of us knowing
We were about to be made whole

A message lied within me
I didn't know where to send it
The product of a breaking heart
And you had come to mend it

At last, I found my purpose
Finally, I knew
The reason I was living
Was all because of you

8-25-2017

BLEEDING PEN (FV)

Trying to find the right words from my bleeding pen.
The ink drips like blood from a fresh wound.
The deep, agonizing cut from wanting to say enough.
What is enough?
Must my heart bleed like the pen that tries to convey a simple message to your very soul?
A message of genuine compassion.
The words need not rhyme.
They have only to cut into you with the same sincerity as they embody when they come from me.
From me & my bleeding pen.
My heart supplies every drop.
And so, I write this question to you.
From the heart, from the mind, to the pen that brings it forth.
What is enough to reach you?

8-25-2017

BLEEDING PEN (THE RHYTHM)

Bleeding pen
I speak through you
Show me what
To say or do

Take my words
That they may grow
That others
May somehow know

I mean them
So sincerely
That I love
Each one dearly

That my words
Were written for
They're someone
I'm praying for

Not just words
I write in vain
Spoken over
Time & again

Bleeding Pen
Don't let me down
Let love be
Forever found

With each word
So carefully
Crafted for
Them willfully

That they may
Be uplifted
To each one
My heart's gifted

Let them see
My love won't end
Craft my words
Oh, bleeding pen

3-2-2017

COMPANION

All my life, for you, I've waited
Starring at clocks
Then our eyes finally locked
To this day, our bond hasn't faded

It's been many years
You're my gift from above
We've shared a pure love
As well as laughter and tears

It seems like yesterday
Though, I'd waited a while
For your beautiful smile
It was worth every step of the way

The skies are bright blue
Though, I didn't choose it
I don't want to lose it
This love that I have for you

I have to tell you or try
May you forever know it
May I not fail to show it
I'll love you til the day that I die

3-6-2017
COMPLETE

I'm not sure what to say
I don't know where to start
I only know that words for you
Lie all inside my heart

Words that can't be spoken
Though some are written down
Even if I tried to say them
I'm not sure they'd make a sound

I'm hoping that you notice
And that you find it sweet
What I mean to say is
That you make my life complete

8-19-2017

DANCING ANGELS

At the waters edge
I find myself
Still and calm

The entire world
Laid out for me
Right in my palm

Just to reach out
And take what I will
As I can

Just to hold it
For 1 brief moment
Within my hand

The sands are white
The grains are many
All is a thought

Sent here by
The voice of God
By only a word was brought

I, too, by a word
Softly spoken
Came here to rest

Finding you, my treasure
Was an added bonus
I'm richly blessed!

As we walk along
I'm reminded
Of days that have passed

Though I look ahead
To times coming
And see what shall last

As a leaf that
Rides the breeze,
Carried by God's wind

Waiting for the spring
And warmth
To begin again

We are carried
On a path together,
One with the other

I gaze upon you
And know inside
There's not another

Not to interfere
Nor to distract
From this constant call

That's alive in winter
Spring, summer
And fall

Maybe onlookers
Stargazers
Who will watch us go

But not 1 soul
Not 1
Will really know

They may speculate
And question
But find no answer

As to the floor
We now stand on
My angelic dancer

As for now we
Wait rather impatiently
For the melody to begin

Til we dance our
Way back home
As one now & again

8-25-2017

DECISION

Though I'm not there
To hold your hand
Don't think that I
Don't understand

What it's like
To be without you
Very few know
As much about you

How you think
How you feel
Those thoughts & fears
You have are real

The concern you have
To make things better
I know as though
You've written a letter

That you've penned
Straight from your soul
To have you home
Is my hearts goal

To see your
Smiling face again
In timelessness
Where love doesn't end

Where the river flows
And there are no tears
Gone are all
Those thoughts & fears

Hold to hope
And cling to God
To stand with me
On Heaven's sod

Make your choice
Don't carelessly roam
A thousand mile journey
Takes a step toward home

8-24-2017
DRIFTING

Carried by the river
Pushed by the breeze
Taken to a space in time
That puts my mind at ease

Sailing in tranquility
Along a winding trail
Aware of my successes
Knowing this won't fail

How far will it take me
How many are the miles
Counting all the stars at night
And seeing all their smiles

As above, so below
Or so I've heard it said
But everything I live for
All rests above my head

And so I'll keep on sailing
Drifting on the wind
Until I find myself back home
And find sweet peace again

8-13-2017

ENTER JAKOB

To climb from distress
A way out of trouble
Their anguish wrapped 'round them
Just like a clear bubble

Though lived by 2
Each felt on their own
Until they met
And made themselves known

They lived separate lives
While sharing one goal
The ultimate dream
Of becoming 1 soul

Joining their portions
And becoming complete
And finally standing
On this souls 2 feet

Days into weeks
Weeks into years
Walking 2 pathways
And facing joint fears

Joining 2 hands
To become 1 mind
To leave this world
And its heartaches behind

Often left wondering
What more could there be
Soon to discover
The 2 would be 3

A peasant & queen
In search of a way
To find themselves
Back home someday

They peered at each other
It was no surprise
To find there was yet
A 3rd pair of eyes

Was it distraction
Or part of their fate
That, indeed, there'd be 3
To pass through the gate

With no need to question
No need to ask why
That they walked on dry ground
With the thirst to fly

The 2 now were 3
That's all that would matter
The twins, the companion
Would climb the great ladder

And press through the gate
Like a bee through the comb
The 3 to be 1
And finally at home

2-23-2017

FINAL STAGE OF LOVE

Say a little prayer for me
To the angels, high above
That my heart will not give in
To this final stage of love

I was diagnosed some time ago
I knew my time was near
I thought I could be stronger
But my strength fell with my tears

They told me I was losing you
They said there was no trying
That one day you'd simply slip away
And that our love was dying

How could I live without you?
How could this ever be?
What could I ever tell them
That I might make them see?

That I'm nothing here without you
Oh lord, what hope have I?
Without your love surrounding me
My heart will surely die

You are all I live for
And what all my dreams are of
Won't you see? Don't let this be
The final stage of love

3-1-2017

FOREVER

Last night I dreamed of you. My sleep was sweet.
I saw myself in a building where fountains flowed & pennies lay shining in the deep waters.
Each penny, a wish someone had made & tossed into a tiny sea.
I wondered what all those wishes could be.
I reached into my pocket & brought out a penny of my own.
I made my wish but was hesitant to toss my coin.
With a deep breath & a moment of silence, I surrendered to the waters that were calling me.
Small circles began forming & expanding as my penny sank into the depths of dreams & fantasies.
And when I looked up, it was hard to see for the tears in my eyes.
I called your name & you appeared.
Long black hair & sparkling brown eyes.
The tiny sea had delivered its promise.
But as I reached to put my arms around you, I found no one there.
A numbness overcame me.
Then I closed my eyes, searched my heart & soul.
It was there I found you forever to be....

8-20-2017

GIFT

No matter how far
Apart we are
We are joined by
The light of 1 star

Your voice echoes softly
On my hearts walls
It soothes & comforts
Each time it calls

When I see your eyes
I see familiar places
Nothing is hidden as they
Shine through empty spaces

Filling the voids
As flood waters moving in
Only freeing me
That new life may begin

You're the light I see
When I open my eyes
A circle of brightness
A constant surprise

A gift to me since
The day you came
You reshaped my life
I'm no longer the same

8-10-2017

GRATITUDE

I'm grateful for the sun
I'm grateful for the rain
Grateful for the pleasure
And even for the pain

Everything I'm grateful for
With all I say & do
Everything up to this point
Has led me back to you

And for that I'm happy
And grateful, all the more
Still grateful for tomorrow
And all it has in store

I'm living in the moment
As I embrace today
Gearing up with gratitude
For what shall come my way

Though grateful for the grey sky
I anticipate the blue
And of all that I am grateful for
I'm thankful most for you

8-20-2017

HEARTS CHAIN

Links like steel
In this chain we make
It may rattle
But will never break

Bound to each other
And will not sever
By knot of 3
Now & forever

It flows like a river
It twists & twines
Made in our hearts
Held in our minds

Strengthening
Yes, day by day
As the shining beam
That lights our way

Scars of our soul
Made times ago
Healed with our minds
As the white light flows

Through triumphs and tragedies
We forever remain
Linked together
In our hearts chain

8-24-2017

HEAVEN ON EARTH

I traveled alone
For more than a score
Not knowing what
I came here for

Searching high
And looking low
Watching
Everywhere I'd go

Then upon
One fateful day
My world would change
In a wonderful way

As a mirror
I was looking in
Something inside
Would begin again

Awakened by
Your eyes & smile
And has lasted
All the while

Everyday
There's something new
That always brings
Me back to you

A newer smile
A fresher word
Like nothing I
Have ever heard

I awake
Each morning to find
Like yesterday,
You're on my mind

And at night
As I have slept
You were in my heart
As always kept

And all along
Throughout my day
You are here
To light my way

My soul inside
Has known since birth
You'd always be
My heaven on earth

8-26-2017

I FOUND YOU

For much longer than I've known you
I knew you were the one
I knew that you were golden
And more radiant than the sun

I knew you were angelic
As celestial as a star
I knew I would do anything
To get to where you are

I knew we would be somewhere
Where we'd never be apart
Then saw we were already there
When I found you in my heart

8-24-2017

ISLAND SWEETS

I sailed away
To a special place
To an island where
I saw your face

On the water
In the sun
From that moment
My trip had begun

With each & every
Wave that crashed
I saw our future
As well as our past

Onward sailing
And onward still
Your heart with mine
I could feel

Though thousands of
Miles behind
I brought you in
My heart & mind

Arriving at
The island fair
The trees were blowing
Like your hair

The sun was shining
Like your eyes
You were there
It was no surprise

As the gulls
Flew gracefully by
For thoughts of you
There was no need to try

Within the wind
Upon the sea
You were
Everywhere with me

As I walked
Atop the sand
The dream to only
Hold your hand

To share this place
And free our cares
To sit with you
Beneath the stars

And count them all
1 by 1
Until our time
On earth is done

Thoughts like these
Consumed my soul
Coming home to you
Became my goal

7 days
Upon the sea
You, in my mind
Were all I could see

Fun was
Everywhere around
But you, my dear
Could not be found

So my time upon
The sea was through
And I made my way
Back home to you

Right where I
Could see your face
For me, there is
No better place

For you, alone
My heart still beats
My paradise
My island sweets

8-24-2017
JUST SO YOU KNOW

You're part of me
Just so you know
You're with me
Everywhere I go

In movies I see
In music I hear
In my heart
You're always near

Never far
But deep inside
Forever, there
You will abide

No one can take me
I won't drift away
I make this promise
To you today

If I should die
Before I wake
No one, from you
Can ever take

This love I have
Will never go
You're part of me
Just so you know

9-3-2017

LIGHTS GO OUT

When the lights came on
I saw your face
But it was your glow
That filled this place

You had a sparkle
You gave a shine
You took your smile
And made it mine

It looked so good
And made me proud
I couldn't speak
My thoughts out loud

Visions & dreams
Filled up my mind
Nothing as sweet
Could I ever find

When night shall fall
You may lose your doubt
I'll still be here
When the lights go out

2-23-2017

LISA

Like a doves wing across the keys
She plays her many melodies
With a kind word & a cheerful smile
She always goes more than a mile

Helping out wherever she can
Guided by His helpful hand
A wife, a sister & nana, too
There's very little she can't do

Appreciated more than she knows
I only hope the gratitude shows
For every little thing she does
No special occasions, just because

Whenever the call, whatever the need
She gives prayer, her time & deed
Handpicked by our Gracious Lord
A faithful servant, much adored

3-6-2017
MORE THAN YOU'LL EVER KNOW

How can I begin to tell you
When there are so many ways
Just how much I love you
And you brighten up my days

There ARE a lot of ways
And I want them each to show
You mean so very much to me
I just want you to know

My mind is always on you
With each passing day & night
Even when I close my eyes
You're still within my sight

I want to say it over
And over yet again
I don't want you to wonder
If my love will ever end

It will go on through eternity
A day & still forever
A love that will not ever fade
And that no one can sever

You will never be forgotten
Though it's hard for you to see
I'll make sure to tell the world
How much you mean to me

And if you should ever wonder
If somehow I've failed to show
Let me tell you that I love you
More than you will ever know

8-25-2017

MR. INDIGO

When you look
Do you see a wall?
Could it be
It's yours to fall?

Do you see
A cloak of wings?
Or do you see
Some other things?

Mr. Indigo
What do you see?
Tell me
When you look at me

When I look at you
I see peace
But, too, a fight
You wish to cease

I see hair of gold
And eyes blue green
And solitude
I've never seen

When I think of you
It's mystery
A fresh face
With no history

I see a man
I see a child
Untamable
Far too wild

Wild like a fire
Yet calm as the sea
I see a soul
That longs to be free

I see old habits
I see affliction
I see the scars
Of past addiction

I see the soul
I see the mind
I see the things
You've left behind

I feel the wind
I see the fire
And beating wings
Climbing higher

A warrior with
A shield & sword
Memories that
You can't afford

To return
And live again
It's time to let
New life begin

The light is shining
On the hill
Close your eyes
And try to feel

A tattered world
You can let go
Rise up,
Mr. Indigo

2-22-2017
MY ROSE

In a garden of thorns
That I never chose
I found amongst them
A single rose

In a sinking valley
I walked each day
This rose grew there
To brighten my way

In the summer heat
Or winter snow
I knew my rose
Would always show

It gave me hope
And inspiration
Like a sort of sacred
Manifestation

In vivid dreams
Or my awakened hour
At anytime
I felt its power

The power of hope
And peace of a dove
It never failed
To show me love

Then in my valley
One day I found
My precious rose
Bowed low, face down

Darkened petals
A faded stem
A duller green
And the red was dim

My garden of thorns
Where my rose had grown
With a sincere love
It had never known...

...Continues to sink
Where no more grows
My ever precious
Sweet, red rose

I long for the day
When on a hill
I find that love
I once could feel
From my valley of thorns
That I never chose
I shall reunite
With my sweet, red rose

9-3-2017

PRAYER FOR YOU

I pray for you
I pray for your peace
My prayers for you
Will never cease

You're on my mind
Not a day goes by
When words fail me
My thoughts still try

To hold your heart
To lift your spirit
With a prayer for you
And God will hear it

When all else fails
I raise through the air
Sending to God
For you, my prayer

2-24-2017

SCAR UPON MY HEART

I remember I was working
You were home, not far
You got hurt at home
I wound up with the scar

The story goes much deeper
Those times were many
If I had money for each time
I'm sure I'd have plenty

But this time stands out to me
We were in different places
And the next day were together
I'll never forget the faces

I showed you my scar
You showed me yours & laughed
The 2 marks were identical
And yet were perfect halves

Everyone around us starred
No one spoke a word
If there had been a pin dropped
For miles it would've been heard

I love all our memories
Every moment shared
But this time will be different
Only one of us spared

I will tell the story
There really is no harm
Only this time the scar
Will not be on my arm

This time you will leave
We soon will have to part
No one will be able to see
The scar upon my heart

3-1-2017

SOUNDS

Sounds.
We take for granted the things we hear.
But when silence is the background and you still hear sounds, it's very real.
Music & laughter, chatter & noise.
It's like seeing snow in the summertime.
You're the only one whose senses are affected.
And so goes the day.
The moment you awake, the sounds begin.
Silence is the background.
Songs and music override the silence.
You open doors and walk from room to room but no radios play.
Going through the day, into the evening, you look forward to night and sleep.
But be assured, when the morning rays pierce your window and you're greeted by the light, there having waited in the silence for you....as you slept, were sounds.

6-17-17

STORY

The night had come
The sun had set
When I'd meet someone
I'd never forget

1 girl left
Another came
They told me,
"You will know her name."

I went to meet her
And as I walked through
Something inside me
Already knew

I looked at her
She looked at me
1 soul in our eyes
Was all we could see

Hour by hour
Day into night
Together we shined
As the sun so bright

The time soon came
She went away
The sun hid its face
From me that day

But the moon still shown
There still was light
Within our hearts
And in plain sight

Several times
We'd meet by chance
The clocks would stop
Their routine dance

Similar health
Similar scars
Similar dreams
Beneath the stars

2 halves of 1 soul
The best of friends
Brother & sister
Yes, even twins

Death would hang
Like a shadow overhead
I lived by every word
That she said

But our bond was strong
And very real
God & this
Would start to heal

Without her
I could not go on
For half my soul
Would then be gone

A year & a half
Would drift away
Til death itself
Would pass away

Untouched, unscarred
Completely clean
The most beautiful shine
I'd ever seen

Her name tattooed
The ink still wet
To show her
I would not forget

Since then, we've shared
A tear, a laugh
And a long overdue
Photograph

A bond like this
I've never known
With anyone
Just she alone

In 22 years
There's much to tell
Countless dreams
I'd never sell

Of my dear friends,
And I love them all
But only 1 has caused
My walls to fall

Who's opened up
My eyes to see
Who broke my chains
And set me free

Half my soul
My heart, my twin
And will be beyond
The day we end

3-6-2017

THANK YOU, LORD

I surrender all
My love to you
With everything
I say & do

I am yours
And yours alone
You are mine,
I've always known

From the moment
That we met
I felt a love
I'll not forget

A forever love
I hold so dear
Within my heart
I find you near

You paid a price
I couldn't afford
With all my heart
I thank You, Lord

2-23-2017

THE CALL

From Genesis to Revelation
To each & every generation
Words of inspiration and hope
To brighten & broaden our scope

Sometimes a story, sometimes a parable
Sometimes personal, always shareable
So that constantly we may
Help others along their way

To help ourselves & others
Making sisters & brothers
Glorifying the Trinity
Becoming one family

That wherever we may go
Letting every person know
Along the way, throughout the ride
He always will be by our side

Trust, obey, always believe
And, oh the joy you will receive
From high & low, near & far
He bids you, "Come just as you are."

8-10-2017

THE WALL

I'm standing in the shadow
Of a great & mighty wall
Behind it you are waiting
We wait to see it fall

It's stood between the 2 of us
Seems like a thousand days
It's time it's been brought down
From standing in our way

It's time we cleared the pathway
We know just what to do
Take down all the obstacles
Separating me & you

Once we were together
Hand in hand we walked
Catching up on years behind us
And, with each other, often talked

Brick by brick, was rising
Between us, this Great Wall
Until it had hid you from me
And was standing there so tall

I've starred at it for years now
Waiting for the time
We could end our separation
And leave this wall behind

Blinded by its shadow
Waiting just to see
As much as I've been missing you
Have you been missing me?

We simply must do something
We've got to say we've tried
Though this wall stands between us
What's in our hearts hasn't died

If it's the last thing that I do
What's lost soon shall be found
I've come to tear down this wall
And leave it scattered on the ground

8-24-2017

TO LOVE YOU

To love you
Is my only task
Not hide this heart
Behind some mask

Not look away
And hide my eyes
What you see
Is no disguise

A heart that glows
Like an autumn moon
And plays a longing
Wishful tune

That upon
Your ears may fall
That you'll know I love you
Once for all

May all souls know
And their eyes see
That you are
Everything to me

As the sun does
Shine above you
I exist
Only to love you

1-31-2017

TODAY

If tonight were my last night
To look to the starry skies
The last time I ever got
To look into your eyes

The last time I had
To see & walk this land
My final opportunity
To take & hold your hand

The last night I would wonder
When I would leave this place
The last chance I had
To look upon your face

All those precious moments
Are in my heart to stay
So also is my love for you
If I should die today

2-23-2017

USE ME

Lord, my life is in your hands
Let it be for Your glory
Let my words speak Your story
May they be part of Your plans

Long after I am gone
May the message still be heard
By a still, undying word
That echoes Your sweet song

And of every generation
From times past & present
And future, be so pleasant
Hope for every situation

With everything I say & do
To heal spiritual blindness
With Your love & kindness
Be not for me, but You

6-21-2017

WATER

While waiting outside
Just looking around
I heard some footsteps
On the ground

The breeze was blowing
Soft that day
The voice of the wind
Had much to say

I turned around
And there to see
Was a stranger
Starring back at me

Expecting the best
Not fearing the worst
He was given water
To quench his thirst

A shine in his eyes
And a smile on his face
He knew he'd found
His sacred space

On that Tuesday
Afternoon
The 7th day
The month of June

Could this familiar face
Unlike another
Possibly be
To me, a brother

Nonetheless
Our conversation
Went beyond
All expectations

Only once before
As best I know
And that was quite
Some time ago

A meeting not
Unlike our own
With another face
My soul had known

A sister then
A brother this day
The spirit knows
No DNA

God knew my prayer
I couldn't sleep
Without asking him
In His safety keep

To place His hand
Above their heads
This was my prayer
These words I said

She had said
The previous day
To help him out
In any way

In her words
I trusted & agreed
Without doubt
Or lack of speed

He asked for water
It was brought down
As we talked
And walked the ground

Such a path I'll walk
Till the day I die
Until the waters
All run dry

3-2-2017
WHAT I FEEL

What I feel when I think of you
Nothing wasted
Memories tasted
Looking to a sunlit sky of blue

Then I feel its heat
The warmth surrounds me
At last, you have found me
I go to a peaceful retreat

I thought of you last night
I grabbed a pen
I tried to begin
But no words good enough to write

Could it have been true
Though my heart didn't stray
I could not find a way
To speak of my love for you?

Still I pressed on
My mind was fighting
To save my writing
It seemed the words were gone

Though I tried hard to say
My words were so futile
I could only but doodle
Til the day had wasted away

Then the morning had come
My thoughts were all OF you
And how much I love you
The words and ink did run

Now as I am laying
May you know I adore you
There's no one before you
I mention your name when I'm praying

May my words form a picture
May they never be blind
To what's on my mind
Which is you, my permanent fixture

2-28-2017

YOU

You are me & I am you.
I see the fear in your eyes.
I feel the warmth of your breath coming toward my face.
I know your anxiety as your eyes move frantically from side to side.
You're as a caged animal waiting for that moment when someone opens the door.
You await your freedom.
Minds like ours are not so rare but that they are joined, is.
I've watched you cry as I looked on helplessly.
I regret that I couldn't take your pain away but I felt it, too.
I've known of your desperate attempts at freedom.
I know the ways you've made hasty decisions at a moments notice & lived to regret them.
I've known when you've drank from that familiar cup, hoping for the madness to stop.
Searching for that bitter pill, praying for escape.
But escape is temporary.
The ride continues & I, as you, keep searching for that switch to stop it.
Anything to break the cycle.
They say that time is of the essence but how much do you have?
Can you endure?
Can you hold on until the end?
You can & you must!
There's no thinking.
Fear as you must, dread as you will.
The ride is not over but with faith you will handle it.
Break the cycle, not the glass.
The smoke will settle & all will be clear again.

I know.
Because
I
Am
You.

4-21-2018
CATS IN TREES

Climbing up
To get a view
And all we see
Is nothing new

All the visions
In the sky
Are identical
To you & I

Patterns & shapes
Of varying sizes
For eyes to break
Their thin disguises

To see what we
Have known for years
The laughter, love
And chill of tears

The stinging bite
Of bitter cold
The inward warmth
Of new & old

The seasons as
They come & go
Each one with
Its unique show

Then we cast
Our sights within
Where we see
Our truest friend

Where I see you
And you see me
In the only place
We're truly free

You're all to me
I can't deny
Like the clouds
High in the sky

As we watch them drift
By on a breeze
With dreaming eyes
Like cats in trees

6-23-2018

CHASING SHADOWS

Shadows move
Across the wall
So many
I can't count them all

Some are black
Some are grey
When night has fallen
Or in the day

Doesn't matter
Where I go
They're with me
So well, I know

More in autumn
And also spring
When time's hands
Have done their thing

Shadows move
Across the sky
Earlier
As days go by

In winter's dark
They seldom cast
Til the equinox
Has come at last

Minute by minute
Day by day
More shadows fall
Across my way

But a truth they know
I know is right
A shadow can't
Produce a light

This truth puts on
A unique twist
Without light
Shadows can't exist

So let them fall
Whenever they may
In deepest night
Or light of day

The sun, the moon
And stars of night
Will chase these shadows
From my sight

6-24-2018
CHOSEN ONE

My love for you is no mistake
Yet it came by as a surprise
I fell for you the moment
That I looked into your eyes

I didn't see it coming
It was like a sudden rain
Ever since it started
I'll never be the same

Each day's a new beginning
More than the day before
So too is every minute
And with each I love you more

Til the day that I lay down
When my time on earth is done
I'll love you even after
And you'll be my chosen one

6-25-2018

DESIRE OF MY HEART

I don't want silver
I don't need gold
I don't need money
And wealth untold

No desire for fortune
No need for fame
Or to see, in lights
My given name

I've traveled to places
And soared through the air
But there's something to this
None can compare

My diamond, my rose
My wish come true
The desire of my heart
Can only be you

You're the wind
Within my sails
You're my comfort
When all else fails

You light the path
I walk each day
And sometimes carry me
Along the way

If I were a song
You'd be the refrain
You are the tracks
For this wandering train

I thank my Lord
For you each night
I cherish you
With all my might

Each day is new
And with you I start
My hope, my dream
The desire of my heart

6-24-2018

EMILY'S FIELD

She dances in the moonlight
By day she lies at rest
Though frequent visits are made
Upon her loved ones quest

The day I came to know her
Is one I won't forget
When she & I became great friends
Before the sun would set

It was a quiet afternoon
With a brother & a friend
A mystery waiting to unfold
And it was all about to begin

My brother in conversation
With the girl he'd come to see
As I sat alone in her living room
Or so I intended to be

I barely heard their talking
But there was something I could hear
The softest voice I'd ever known
Was whispering in my ear

Gradually, it strengthened
I wondered, "What it could be?"
Then I stood to my feet & asked the girl
"Who is Emily?"

The eyes of this girl were bright
With a look of disbelief
This woman that I'd called by name
Was a subject of her grief

Emily was her great aunt
Who'd passed before the birth of this girl
Funny that she talked to me
This day, in our own world

Her hair was straight and long
Her eyes a shade of brown
And when I heard her voice that day
It was a lovely sound

This girl & I went riding
Along a country trail
On our way to see Ms. Emily
And to see proof of this tale

We walked up to her graveside
Where a yellow rose had grown
It was a bittersweet experience
To kneel beside her stone

Knowing I was with friends
One of whom just revealed
I'll never forget that afternoon
I visited Emily's field

6-22-2018

FINAL CHAPTER

Beneath dim lights, I sat
Looking around the room
In every eye there was a tear
Glistening in the gloom

Light chatter and conversations
Were all that could be heard
Then silence overcame the crowd
As we waited for the Word

Words in song preceded
With a message of hope to share
Of a comforting thought to ponder
"Won't It Be Wonderful There?"

To children and loved ones in sorrow
Whose minds were on one who had gone
The dear preacher spoke with compassion
Of the truth that we each should pass on

He spoke of a loving Father
Who abides beyond the sky
Who for the sake of His dear precious children
Sent the one son he had to die

This Christ would come down to our dwelling
And for everyone of us here
Would stretch out his arms & shed all his blood
Without hesitation or fear

3 days after Christ was exhausted
And in a tomb that was sealed by the wise
Would make of them fools in an instant
When from this grave he'd arise

Just as he said this would happen
As it's written and so it is done
Eternity is awaiting
For all who will come to the Son

Each life here is a book
When we're born, the pages turn
Each page as we live it
With a lesson we must learn

From cover to cover are we
Into chapters our book is divided
'Less the book that we are be burned,
In his library, we will be united

As a page that's within your fingers
Your life, by his breath, has been stirred
Remember your books final chapter
Is not finished til he gives his word

6-25-2018
I'M LOVING YOU

As by some sort of accident
I first laid eyes on you
But I knew I wasn't dreaming
Nor was it too good to be true

Your dark eyes seemed to shine
Your smile was ever bright
The moon and stars were irrelevant
It was you who lit my night

Glowing like a rainbow
In magnificent silver and gold
I felt you were an angel
And then I watched your wings unfold

But I can't get over that smile
Unexaggerated nor fake
Just a simple thought about you
Sweet one, my breath you take

6-11-2018

IF LOVE WAS JUST A COLOR

If love was just a color
What color would you see?
Would that color come from you
And radiate to me?

Would it pass right by me
As though I wasn't there?
Like a stick of incense,
Would it permeate the air?

Would your color then surround me
And cloak me with a veil
Then motion me to follow it
Along a beaten trail?

I'd walk your colored pathway
No doubt I'd find my way
I'd follow dusty colors
To be with you everyday

We'd soak up sun together
With our colors intertwined
Lighting up the space around us
While emptying our minds

Then filling with one color
As the shadows we evade
Replacing them in harmony
With the color we have made

Siblinghood & friendship are
The colors that I'd see
If love was seen in color
It would shine through you and me

5-21-2018
KEEP ME AWAY

Standing in the doorway
I was taken by surprise
My life flashed before me when
I looked into your eyes

When you stood before me
I was taken by your light
Though the sky was void of stars
That stormy, summer night

Bright bolts lit the sky
Thunder sounded loud
Alone, were we, near by the rain
Yet lost within a crowd

Each with a light inside us
Ready to be shown
2 flames to burn together
From a fire, since birth, we've known

God brought us together
As He'd promised us one day
All hell cannot divide us
Or, from you, keep me away

6-26-2018

OUR DESTINY

My sister, the Scorpio
And I, the Taurus
Await the destiny
That lies before us

As 2 we came
As 1 we'll leave
Our minds know
Our hearts believe

Wanderers, seekers
Abilities unique
Our perfection is coming
As we reach the peak

The mountain is ready
The moon is bright
Could be anytime
Maybe tonight

The time approaches
Regardless the hour
When we're summoned by
The Higher Power

As lightning bugs
Kept in jars
When the lids open
We'll join the stars

Like a single light
Within the sky
It's natural
No need to try

Twins below
One soul above
In the land
Of perfect love

No more sickness
No more pain
We'll ride the wind
Without a plane

What we have within
Needs no remedy
We lie in wait
Our certain destiny

5-20-2018

OUT OF MY HANDS

The hour glass is running
I cannot stop its sands
As I can't stop my love for you
It is out of my hands

Watching birds in flight
As to their homes they go
As my home lies inside your heart
My emotions for you flow

Like a waterfall that never ends
More love comes from behind
Falling ever for you
You're all that's on my mind

You're all that's in my heart
With every beat, it's true
This world would've had no place for me
If it hadn't been for you

The earth would stop its turning
The moon would cease to gleam
My sun would never shine again
Without you, my dream

I stand in wait to act upon
Each of your hearts demands
As my heart pours out its love for you
That's eternally out of my hands

6-24-2018

ROSES IN CHAINS

A bond that can't be broken
A love that will never die
No sea exists too wide
Nor a mountain rise too high

To keep us from each other
Or to ever come between
Whether on a city sidewalk
Or in wide fields of green

We walk this world together
No separation will come
Until the place where we are going
From where we have come from

No floods to rise around us
To fires to burn us down
When everything has settled
2 hearts will still be found

Whether it be in this world
Or in Heaven's starry plains
Forever 2 as 1
We are roses in chains

6-20-2018

SEA OF TEARS

Warm as the morning sun
Cooler than the rain
Sometimes without feeling
Sometimes filled with pain

Mostly when I think of you
Sometimes I can laugh
Always with your memory
Enough to light my path

Which leads me back to you
My tears back to the sea
My heart to the beginning
Of the start of you and me

To a night I saw you crying
Missing someone dear
Though difficult to feel much pain
Because we were so near

Close to one another
Physically and in heart
In spirit and in mind
This bond won't break apart

Just knowing you are hurting
Always gets the best of me
I'll be the strength you need
While my tears fill up the sea

5-26-2018

SOMEONE

You are my someone
That I breathe and live
You are what I'm here for
And with all my heart I give

My tears, my joy, my laughter
All I hold inside
All of me is part of you
Until the day I die

But what then, you ask
That's easy to explain
We join our hearts together
Like cars of a train

Linked together always
As on this journey we go
With just one destination
Yes, just one place to go

On this path together
Wherever it may lead
I'll have no want for anything
You are all I need

So take my hand, let's go
It's all we're dreaming of
Forever through eternity
Be my someone to love

6-27-2018

SOMEONE LIKE YOU

Not everyone can see it
Not everybody knows
That within a garden of weeds
I found you, my rose

The melody I sing to
The beauty that I see
Like coffee in the morning
You're so many things to me

The first thought that I go to
To ease my troubled mind
The compassion that is needed
When this world is so unkind

My light within the darkness
My prayer down on my knees
If life were a prison
You would be my keys

I wish all people felt this
That everybody knew
How wonderful life would be
If they had someone like you

5-21-2018

THE JOURNEY HOME

I dreamed of you all night last night
We talked up until dawn
I dreamed we made our journey
From all this, we were gone

I saw you, I heard you
I felt your presence close
It was more than just a dream
It was what we wanted most

We relived days of work
Then began to run a maze
Searching for escape from chaos
Into better, brighter days

Gifts we had manifested
New talents came to light
This vision we shared continued
2 or 3 times last night

Within it, detailed facts
As your spirit came to me
Teaching to me patience
And to rise above. Be free!

The talk, the dream, the living
All that we'd come to know
Was all about to change
The time would come to go

You handed me the wages
The attendant I would pay
For us to board the bus together
And so be on our way

You were a little ahead of me
I caught up pretty fast
We were aboard with others like us
And were on our way, at last

The last thing I remember
The last thing I could see
Was looking in your eyes
And you were smiling back at me

This reflection of our hearts
This painting on our wall
Of a Journey we live eternally
And I don't mind at all

One day we will awaken
Inside Heavens dome
To find the ride was not in vain
And our love has brought us home

6-28-2018

PAPER FLOWERS

Many years we've waited
For countless days & hours
Sifting through the sands of time
Gathering paper flowers

From times that have long since passed
To the present that we see
Always fully knowing just
How much you mean to me

In a so imperfect world
Toward a future so unsure
Looking back I know we have
The strength left to endure

We've faced so many obstacles
And walls along the way
Yet we've conquered them together
Becoming stronger, day by day

Someday we'll reach our destiny
Where all our dreams are true
With no more paper flowers
Just fresh roses picked for you

Milton Keynes UK
Ingram Content Group UK Ltd.
UKHW040237031224
451863UK00001B/110